A DROP OF WISDOM

Contents

Introduction..4

Thought..12

Emotions...38

Who Am I...58

The Creator...74

The Soul..80

The Life Force....................................87

The Realms of Existence....................99

Auras & Chakras..............................112

Meditation..133

The Theory.......................................151

The Drop of Wisdom.......................162

Introduction

It has been said: "in the beginning there was nothing there was a void a timeless, space-less, nothingness; and to this nothingness came a purposeful thought, and it filled the void... In the beginning there was an eternal thought, and for thought to be eternal, time must exist. So into the all purposeful thought grew the law of time."

Perhaps you think this is just another book; there have been a lot of discussions about spirituality, where some people find it confusing and hard to understand. Well it is a complicated subject, but when I decided to write this book I thought I would simplify it as much as possible, at the same time delivering the knowledge in an organized fashion. Step by step, we will build a foundation that will bring about the man of wisdom. You have to do your work, but you will know where to start and what to do. "Seek, and you shall find".

What is Spirituality but the attainment of the higher purpose of the self in this universe.

Is it the way to understand the world that was created before us in a unique way?

Are our encounters connected to simple life choices that we make, and would the understanding of these choices bring about who we are on the spiritual scale?

In living life to the fullest we will find the positive and goodness in everything we do; we will put forth a good karma that will ripple through the universe that something is still good. Is there someone echoing the sound of a new age where we all can be what we want to be; is that you man of wisdom?

This attainment might take months, years, decades, and even lifetimes; time doesn't matter but what really matters is the living of a spiritual life that will bring you to the greatness you are meant to be. The thing about spirituality is that if you don't discipline yourself it will never be attained, and these disciplines will change your body, mind and heart. What gives to all that, but the true meaning of life and understanding of the mind and the works of the heart; when these concepts work together they will bring a new thinking a new understanding a new level to be filled by you, the true man of wisdom.

Most of the religious views and philosophical thoughts have had an effect in bringing on the light on to our humanity; they have tried to define faith, God, belief, how we think, how to behave, how to thrive, and who we are as individuals, society, family, and country and they have successfully shined a good light on spirituality, knowing God, life after death and gave us a beautiful view of who we are in this universe and the purpose of us as a continuing learning experience.

Contemplating all these thoughts into one big working system that people must achieve in order to understand life, God, and our selves; this spiritual understanding is a big step and a huge leap forward to create more great minds in the advancements of spirituality.

In these days everyone is looking for some kind of spiritual guidance; some have found it in religion which their parents before them have followed; some have followed a teacher or a guru; some did their own research and developed their knowledge, and many more experiences from life and interactions with people that lead them to a good place in the spiritual understanding, but if you don't know where to start, how are you going to build this strong foundation of belief that will set you on the right path.

Like a pyramid your belief should be. The pyramid is a very strong building it almost can withstand anything and this is how your belief and your understanding should be; your heart and your mind must work together in order to achieve the higher purpose of your life.

I am writing this book in an effort to build a constructed guide which will help the reader in understanding the basic concepts of spiritual fundamentals.

We all are subject to religion, race, region, the society we live in, the family that we grow up with, the traditional values and our doctrines that was taught to us from an early age. From these subjections we have been lead the way of the sheep; all actions taken in the social and religious organization must be followed blindly regardless of the reaction or repercussions and even the rights of one's person. You have been imprisoned and its time for you to break free and become the UNLIMITLED potential. These conducts are just the means of control of one's mind or limiting the ability of any human to stay lesser, and in doing so he is subject to the will of others just like the sheep. These limitations makes the man of wisdom to be, never be... this control hinders or slows down the emanation of more great minds, and this will hinder the society towards spiritual advancement; which in its way will hinder humanity in a big way in spiritual and mind progress.

A lot of people are influenced by the religious leaders that crave power; which they fail to understand that each of us has their own unique experience that must be accepted as it is, and each experience is a book on its own, or a story on its own in the bible of life. Each of us has a unique ability that we bring to the table; these reforms must be nourished so we can bring the change that will shape the life we are living.

Every soul is precious beyond imagination and working together makes the whole, WHOLE. So fighting each other will only hinder our growth and our survival as a WHOLE.

We have to grow out of this ignorance, and out of these dark thoughts and move toward the fire of light of spiritual wisdom. We live in these bodies; which they are the vessels to our souls, to be given the opportunity to become the greatest version of our selves. So what's stopping you from becoming the man of wisdom, but you?

Working together and helping each other to attain the truth is our biggest game changer. The knowledge that I have, it didn't come all of a sudden; it took years of study and experimentation and research and open mindedness to all possibilities and opportunities and I tell everyone to always do their research and experiment and conclude with their mind and understand it; I only give examples just to give my prospective idea on my experiences, but always allow your mind to do the understanding. Even if your conclusion was lacking at this time; there will be a time when you will learn the bigger picture, and how all it fits together; this just means that you're not ready for that specific level; always keep an open mind to change the stuff you have learned in the past, because when you learn you expand your mind, and in doing so it expands your consciousness in to the real wisdom and deepens your knowledge into the mystery of spirituality. The deeper the rabbit hole goes the more fine the knowledge becomes, how far are you willing to dig?

Have you ever wondered why we are here?

Well this book tries to answer some of the logistic questions of why we seek the unseen and the fact that mystery always gets to our heart and soul in a way we don't expect it. It will provide some of the answers that seekers of truth try to understand; it will help you be involved in the spiritual work that will bring you to a higher degree of knowledge and spirituality; which is required of you to attain a higher state of consciousness.

Why is everything the way it is?

Why do we suffer?

Why do we die?

Is there a creator or everything is just random?

Is there a grand plan for me, or I make the best of it?

I have often asked myself these questions.

All these questions can only be answered philosophically, because if you don't experience with your mind and heart they cannot be comprehended, and you will not know. You can't just get the answers from a book, a movie, a teacher, or a guru; the spiritual involution and evolution can suppress it or expand it. All knowledge can come from within and from without if you have the key.

If you have a group of people and none of them have ever tasted a grape, and you're trying to explain what a grape would taste like; you cannot describe it, not even if you used a million words. Let them taste the grape and feel it and they will know it themselves.

Life is too short to experience everything, but you have to focus on what you are meant to do here at this moment in this life time, and learn from this experience as much as you can; every day brings a new lesson and every lesson has a purpose and the man of wisdom is the one to know it.

I am not a seer, and I am definitely not a prophet; I am just a man who tapped into the unknown and was shown a lot more than he bargained for. The more I learnt the more I knew that there is more to know. So I would like to show my fellow seekers some of these things that I have experienced; we all need help sometimes and advancing spiritually is especially hard. We can't all go through the same experiences, but we can surely learn from each other's experiences as we all graduate.

It is hard when you are stuck, or don't know even where to start, or even to understand something that's beyond you; that's why we are all here. We all can help each other in advancing spiritually and mentally and become the masters of our minds.

Thinking what religion you are and thinking that you are "the chosen people of GOD", and thinking that you are right and everyone else is wrong is just such low level of thinking and pure ignorance. Every religion out there is a part of the bigger puzzle of the whole, and each one is so important that it cannot be omitted or taken lightly otherwise we will all fail. Imagine a society that has the thought of one big happy family in this universe; if you come to see that nothing is evil and there is nothing dark and there is nothing cold; where for evil is the absence of good and darkness is the absence of light and cold is the absence of heat then what we are left with is how much goodness do we have in us?

Understanding this spiritual side of things is very important to practice and implement it into our daily lives, and do our share to awaken as many minds as possible, but what is more important than that or as important is to do all this from the heart not because you have to but because you want to. It's a new era, a lot of wars are happening and the greedy getting greedier and the poor is getting poorer and everything feels like it is circling down the drain. No you will never fail unless you stop trying its always going to be hard, but our choices and actions determine who we really are and what we really stand for and what we fight for. Is it money? Is it power? Or is it freedom? Or is it just a feeling, feeling cannot be taught

cannot be bought and it is just incredible.
Without feelings we become robots..... To awaken the real
you; you must experience the feeling of things around you,
through your mind and your heart.

Everyone has something to offer the rest of us. If you have
doubts in that don't worry you just haven't discovered it yet.
It doesn't necessary mean on a Grand scale, but someone in
your life will come along and will need your help ,so... are
you going to help them or not?

I am a spiritual seeker, a truth knower; I have climbed from
the depth of ignorance coming forth into light, with fire in my
soul and love in my heart and consciously moving forward
unhindered. Free willed and focused I come forth to give this
book to the people who need it in the hope to help anyone
who seeks it.

"Ascension, with us it starts and with us it will continue until
we become the man of wisdom."

Thought

The quest in which we all thrive to accomplish is to achieve higher wisdom, and to ascend into a higher purpose with the understanding of all that is; with this understanding we become so much more than just a living being, but we become the living essence of a mind that has been shaping our understanding of all the things that is in existence.

With every subject of discussion the sole purpose is the understanding of even the most basic level of its comprehension, because in order to build upon basics we must conceive the knowledge that comes forth in an organizational way; in doing so we are always prepared to receive more knowledge and expand our consciousness without risking the shake of the whole foundation. When an idea or a thought presents itself and we are not capable of fitting it into our system of belief; it may do more harm than good. In most of esoteric traditions, there is always a period where the initiates must go through a search of self love and self knowing before they can be inducted to continue their higher learning.

Here comes the first lesson of thought which is one of the most important subjects of all time. It dazzled the scientists, philosophers, religious leaders and thinkers of all the ages with its complexity and incomprehensiveness; to have tasted something so complicated can leave people helpless and baffled of the extremity of such things existing, but to our benefit we have a mind to conceive our mind.

How the human brain works, behaves, and how thought is formed in the most formidable way; every action you take is derived from a thought and every thought can manifest an action. Many books have been written on the subject but still couldn't cover every situation or manifest every thought.

It is natural for the reader to understand at least how thought is manifested and how the brain works; when you understand this subject even on the basic level then every situation that presents itself to the reader should fall in the basic structure of the building block of understanding. In doing so, you don't have to read every book on thought to understand thought you just have to know the basics. When you read more to further your experience in this field you will have insight into that same subject of experience. Without the basic concept of the thought process, the understanding becomes corrupted and not organized.

Each thought is a piece of the puzzle no matter how complicated the puzzle is, it has its formal place and it shouldn't change. Disarray will only scatter your conscious thinking and you will fail your quest.

The first chapter will prepare the reader to wet their feet in the sea of knowledge readying them to test the water in order to take on the big unknown. To recognize where you stand gives you the realization of self importance and the necessity to start the quest on becoming the man of wisdom.

Whatever your beliefs are you must build them on a good foundation. The foundation should be built like a pyramid where the structure will hold itself by itself; every time you add to the structure it becomes a part of the whole not separate from it. In order to succeed in this build you must think of the whole as one unit; as earth is a part of our solar system, as the solar system is to the whole Milky Way, and the Milky Way is to the universe and so on and so forth. This pyramid structure of your mind must be strong and able to with stand the assaults of the outside world's delusions and misinformation.

Where do you stand in the degrees of spirituality compared to the rest of the universe?

In defining and understanding the subject of thought we would have put forth the basic stepping stone of the great work of spirituality, and the start of a great journey in becoming the man of wisdom.

What Are Thoughts?

There are many different kinds of thought that we encounter on daily bases. Some of these thoughts come naturally without the process of thinking in a form of an automatic conscious response, and some need focused unhindered attention, and some become routinely semi focus semi automatic. You have to understand that even though the brain holds all the neurons and functions it is the mind that is in control of the brain. The mind and the brain are different and I will explain both later in this chapter, but first what are these kinds of thought:

1. When a familiar action takes place from a recall, or to remember details of an event that happened we call this type of thought the memory. It contains most of the thoughts that are saved up from every encounter in your life. Your mind always picks automatically which to save, but you can train to save whatever you like as long as you will it to be.

2. In our daily life we will encounter many events some will be pleasant and easy enough to go through, while others will produce problems that we have to overcome and concur; this type of thought is called logic; it is the core of problem solving of our day to day activity, and it is often in conflict with feelings and emotions.

3. When danger arise and we are not prepared for it; a thought will surface that will induce a series of actions that you aren't aware of nevertheless it is executed automatically; this type of thought is called instinct. Since everything happens in the mind you can't overlook that instinct is not just a gut feeling, but it had to have its acting impeded in the root of the mind.

4. Innovation is one of the most popular of thought. We are always creating no matter how small the activity is; we are always in motion into new realities or even finding new ideas to fix problems permanently.

5. The belief that was pushed on to you since you were a baby. This type of thought is very delicate, because most of the populous is entangled in it or hindered by it; it is very hard to open your mind and accept new ideas if you are firm or stubborn in

this belief. The big problem in our society is that what people expect of you and how are you suppose to think that is subjugated thought. It's time to break free and unleash your potential.

6. The learning thought is the best tool to gain knowledge and unlock the potential. It is close to the memory but the way of absorbing the knowledge differs; you have to pour your thought into the essence of that you want to learn and when you pull it out again you would have acknowledged the presence of something new; as if you wrap your thought around the idea and dissolve it in your mind. This type of thought differs from one person to another; the gaining depends on the pyramid structure of the person's competence toward education and how well the understanding can be fitted to the structure of the mind.

There are other types of thought that we will not concentrate on here, but we have to mention that every thought is important and there is a lot more than I have stated here, but we will suffice with the ones I have brought forward for self developing purposes...

Process of Thought

Before any action can occur a thought must manifest. The process in which this will take place is concentrated into two major parts. These two major parts will play one of the biggest roles into understanding spiritual wisdom; they are the back bone of the entire knowledge criteria of philosophical and spiritual development. The two major parts of the thought process are as follows:

A) The brain:

Since the dawn of time, there have been always developments in the structure of our brain. The brain is the physical part that is housed in the skull, and it's ever changing and becoming more sophisticated and rewired with every idea that is introduced to it. As we progress through our evolution of existence our brain continues to evolve to fit our daily needs and advance in accordance to our survival.

There are scientific studies nowadays suggest that the brain is always changing ever rewiring itself with every thought. Every time you acquire new thought the brain rewires itself through a process called Neuroplasticity which the brain creates new neurons to fit the idea with the rest of the belief that we have or the build of our thought. This is why a pyramid structure learning method will serve you greatly on the long run.

The brain is the most important tool that you will ever need to use to observe the physical manifestations that is around you. When you look with your eyes the cornea transfers the image to the brain via neurons; the brain in its function analyzes and produces information of that image that we see in our process of input. Same happens in hearing, touching, smelling, and tasting each taking on a task for us to input on the world around us. None of this is possible without the brain; the brain leads the functions of all the physical body in an organizational way; where we cannot comprehend but always thriving to understand.

The brain is the central processing manager of the whole body. It holds the neurons with all the body parts communicating with each other through the conduit "the brain".

The brain takes care of irregular muscle functions; these irregular muscles are responsible for our survival and they work together with the brain without our command or our awareness of their functions. We don't command our heart, lungs, kidneys, liver, and pancreas, etc... to work; the brain automatically does all this for us without even us knowing about any of them at work.

The muscles that are under our command like hands and legs are our tools that our brain uses under our conscious aware self to execute actions commanded by us to our brain; where the brain brings the command to our muscles in order to execute the desired action, and the purpose behind every movement and muscle manipulation we come to do is through our brain.

As we will discuss that the brain is the conduit of the mind; the mind asserts its presence on the physical world through the brain. Yet the absence of the brain means the physical body dies, but the mind thrives on in another vessel; where the absence of the mind means the brain is a zombie; we must realize that the mind is connected to all that is where the brain is the tool and that the mind uses the brain to complete its tasks.

B) The mind:

What defines us from other forms of life is the presence of a magnificent ever expanding everlasting ever evolving essence we call "the mind". The mind is the non physical part that we call conscious and sub conscious surrounding and inhabiting our brain.

The very purpose of our mind is to grow consciously. The ultimate goal is to attain the cosmic conscious mind, graduate from the school of life and death, and become the man of wisdom.

Each one of us has his mind connected to the higher mind of all or the first mind; we call this mind the cosmic mind. The connection between the cosmic mind and our own mind is what gives us the external sense of spirituality and the purpose of existence; to have this connection strong or conscious means that we have a higher degree of spirituality. Just like a cable, the thicker the cable the more current of electricity can go through and vice versa if the cable was smaller. That means lesser connection to the higher conscious cosmic mind the lesser is the spiritual degree of that person. The cosmic mind knows how your connection is; there are some points for this issue of connecting where karma, knowledge, devotion, and love are the four that will connect you to the cosmic mind and to the rest of the creation. Your experience and the interactions to all that is will set the guide for your connectivity with the cosmic mind; working on your betterment in these fields will raise you up on the spiritual scale and will put forth the good understandable communication between you, the cosmic mind and the rest of the creation.

Your mind holds the potential of expanding your consciousness to a limitless degree; our thoughts are created in our mind with the help of the cosmic mind. The cosmic mind contains all the wisdom and knowledge there is to be, but one "the idea of God".

When a thought is created by the mind it moves into the physical brain and envelopes it. When this happens the brain goes to work and see how the brain can relate to that thought; the brain seeks any information about the thought in the memory, and will either process it forward or discard it. If the thought was carried through we will visualize it to become a real idea in our brain which in its own accord will bring it into creation on its own, whatever it is math, art, politics, work, etc....

We are what we think, and what we think we become; with our mind we shape our thoughts, and with our thoughts we make our world. Whatever your mind sends to the cosmic mind, the cosmic mind sends it back with affirmation; when you send positive thoughts you get back positive manifestations, and when you send negative thoughts you will get back negative manifestations. When your brain is in a positive state of emotion from your heart (intent is everything in this), your mind picks up on these emotions and these emotions will affect the untrained mind, and these thoughts will be sent to the cosmic mind; the cosmic mind looks about this thought in a state of how positive or how negative it is and the visualization comes affirmatively responsive to the will of the thinker or the thought sender; the cosmic mind will send a representation of that thought onto the physical world as an impulse forcing itself into the world.

Boundaries of Thought

It has been scientifically proven that thought exist as a wave and it is measurable in cycles per second or hertz. Through the advancement in science we have been able to categorize thought into different frequencies where our encounters with the physical world provide the acknowledgment and definition for these waves we call thoughts. Furthermore we can categorize these thoughts and define where they stand in the mind as a wave. The investigation toward understanding the brain and the mind is at hand and since we know the difference between the mind and the brain we can define the thought waves:

1. **The delta wave**: It is a wave measuring between 1 to 3 hertz. This frequency wave is produced when the brain is in a sleep state where dreams occur; this is the calmest state which the brain can be in.
2. **The theta wave**: It is a wave measuring between 4 to 8 hertz. This frequency wave is produced when the brain is in deep relaxation, lucid dreaming, and state of bliss or meditation. It's a good healing wave; this is the state of most relaxing while still awake.
3. **The alpha wave**: It is a wave measuring between 9 and 13 hertz. This frequency wave is produced when the brain is in his wakeful normal state of daily functions; this is when the brain is relaxed not doing much thinking, but fully conscious; this is a state of balance no anxiety no stress not happy not sad just right or neutral.
4. **The beta wave**: It is a wave varies a lot it has a wide range between 13 to 30 hertz. Our brain is fully alert, moving, thinking and learning we spend most of our time in this wakeful very alert state of focus; this frequency wave is produced when you are doing your

daily job, driving, socializing, learning, etc...This is the best state to be in for learning.

5. **Other waves**: There are waves that are higher than these in the state of mind; these waves will put the brain into the survival mode, anxiety, fear, anger, and blood lust. Here the mind is unpredictable and under the influence of emotional manipulations.

Note: hertz mean a cycle / sec

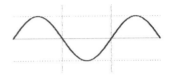

These states of mind are very important to understand, because what the brain does the body always follows, and what the mind puts forth the brain will execute. If you can control your thoughts your mind will bend to your will and all that follow; for example there are some monks that can control their breath and slow down their heart beat to 1 beat / min and stay alive; I would call that mind over matter.

The mind operates differently than the brain where the mind is of the spiritual not of the physical and consist of many layers; each layer has its own function and purpose, and each has a part of the whole that is important for the whole and any missing part of the whole will make it incomplete; incomplete mind might result in a lot of dysfunctions in the brain and that could lead to insanity or other behavioral dysfunctions. An incomplete mind will decrease the grip on understanding the world and anything that is in it; the focus of the mind will be solely to the belief that it is stuck on. The brain will suffer from this state and produce multiple personality disorder, no remorse murders, or any unexplainable evil doings. This state will lead to incompletion of the quest or the task that should have been carried on this life time; a similar life test will occur to achieve the alternative result that is needed to surpass this life time's quest, which was missed in this life time. Dealing with the mind is very dangerous and delicate; at the same time it is very important to recognize that the state of the mind will set the stage for the advancement in spirituality. In the betterment of your mind you can change your world and become the man of wisdom.

The prospect of understanding and the prospect of observing can go hand in hand and sometimes dependant on each other; I observed while I was meditating that the simplification of this subject down to the "pizza sauce" making can help understand while observing, where the entirety of the spiritual world can be broken down so we can understand it piece by piece and relate it all to the whole; the only thing is finding the real information that can give the right division where to start in this quest, and I noted to myself; the pizza sauce for a person eating a pizza is just a sauce, but for the cook it is so much more; it is the tomatoes and the herbs and spices and so much more stuff that all need to be right every time. The consumer does not need to know what goes in the pizza sauce, but he wants a good tasting pizza; if we say that the pizza sauce is spiritual understanding, that makes the man of wisdom the pizza sauce maker; he does not create anything but he uses the right things in the right place. Unfortunately most of us are but consumers in the spiritual world instead of making the spiritual world work for us. If the spiritual world became known to us, and we knew what it is, how it works and where we are on that map we can walk the path of consciousness and climb the ladder of knowing. We can become not only the consumers but the apprehenders of the whole as it is.

The layers of the mind

Understanding the mind is very complex; we have to define every layer and uncover the purpose of each one.
You must define what you need to work on, and what to omit and how to improve.
The layers of the mind are like an onion wrapping where all the layers are confined and twined on top of the other; each layer is linked to all the rest and all work as one to complete the cycle of understanding and action.

The purpose of each layer is embedded in the state of the conscious mind where it resides at every level; as if the conscious mind is the dial where the selective interface of the conscious is wrapped in that layer. The conscious mind exists on every level as if it is the heart of the onion where all connect to the outside world through the conscious. Before defining the layers of the mind we need to recognize that the conscious is a part of the mind, but at the same time it is the output of the mind to the physical world.

The layers of the mind are as follows:

1. **The Self:**
    It is the spirit of one's personal intellect where the accumulation of all your past lives that happened is impeded into one. We will discuss the self later in this work; I will suffice with this explanation for now, and that mastering the self will discipline your mind.

2. **The Subconscious:**

    It is the part of the mind that tries to understand and

make sense of feelings; the subconscious works with the conscious mind, the self, and the cosmic mind because feelings run on every level; since feelings are so complex to understand the mind needs something that operates in that domain of complexity to understand the feelings that are flooding in where the automatic responses of the subconscious is the true conduit of understanding the feelings.

To apply any feeling to the conscious mind, the subconscious tries to illustrate the feelings as images or symbols of their representation as they come to the conscious mind; here the conscious mind will understand it in his logic. We can now have an idea of what we feel and how we feel it from the heart by our subconscious.

To operate on these levels the subconscious must have access to all of the layers where the subconscious is the grounding figure of the mind where everything is felt; every possible experience must be handled by the mind at the conscious state, but the subconscious is where all the experiences are felt. (The conscious gets his share of the experiences only when operating in the wakeful state, while the subconscious operates on all layers of the mind, the conscious is like the outer layer of the subconscious). The subconscious sees dreams, instinct, and intuitiveness before introducing it to the conscious; creativeness of our entire world is the outcome of our subconscious, and all aspects of our life are in our subconscious. Here is the rub you cannot access your subconscious willingly unless you have mastered your will; the subconscious communicates with us in a very unique way using symbolism (symbolism here means the illustration of things through other means), because the subconscious cannot make words of explanation.

Pay attention to your dreams, because most of your dreams are in your subconscious trying to tell you something you need to work on or something you need to pay attention to, or even comforting you on some level, but all these dreams are nothing if you don't know what they mean. Dreams illustrate all the information as close to life like as it makes sense. The sub conscious mind processes the information with symbols in order to give the message a meaning or a purpose; what these symbols represent at that time to the subject is the real concept of the dream. The concept of dreaming is to take into consideration that what the dreamer is seeing (all in codes, for example: if you see water does not necessarily mean water, but maybe a body of emotions) and what does it mean, and how they feel at that moment in the dream. Dreams could illustrate many things like psychological behavior or mistreats to concepts or situations the mind keeps dwelling on and can't get past them. There is a reason for every dream and it is up to you to find out what they mean.

Our subconscious is the window in which we see the world of the ether; when we start to understand the meaning behind what our subconscious mind is telling us; we will see the ether world to what it really is. The trained disciplined mind can achieve the understanding of these visions and dreams; this accomplished seeker tends to decipher the code and put them in to use where it is needed. To achieve this level of mastery of your mind might take many lifetimes, but if you work hard and understand what you are learning while implementing them into your daily life you will grow inch by inch on to wisdom and become the disciplined man of wisdom. The man of wisdom is the man that knows his place amongst the stars, he knows who he is in the kingdom of nature, and he will understand the ether world and beyond.

To will your mind is the very act of becoming the master of thy self; the will is the very act of manifestation onto the world, and the only way to be the master of your will is through the discipline of the body and emotions through the mind. Unlocking the potential where the subconscious resides is one of the keys to act upon this world with your will and not your emotions, and always remember that your emotions are the motive and not the actual act.

3. The Animal Self:

It's a part of the actual self, but yet separate on the lower scale of the mind. We have this common with the animals (animals have this as their whole mind. only animalistic no other layers exist or residing in their mind otherwise). It is the ability to know the things around us, to thrive for survival and have the ability to defend the self in nature. This part of the mind is very aggressive and egoistic also it is the warrior and the protector; the animal self is very important to the mind yet is uncontrollable, but through the will.

Senses serves the animal self for procreation and

other means of survival; the down fall of that side or the negative aspect is that it is induced and infused with seduction and temptation for all that is physical. When the conscious mind is in this state, all things of temptations and physical needs of satisfactory to the self will overcome any other intellectual properties and only the desires stay. The self must be trained and disciplined for it to conquer the desire of the animalistic self and prevent the self from becoming ever close to the animalistic self, yet consciously leaving the animal self for use, because it is needed never the less.

It is safe to say that the animal self is very important for survival, but at the same time we have to distinct between survival and being ruled and maneuvered by the animal self. We have to put our self above the animal self in order for us to grow spiritually and be on our way in becoming the man of wisdom.

The animal self is:
   a) The survival mind.
   b) The animalistic nature with all its attributes.
   c) The preservation and protector mind.
   d) The aggressive mind (anger).
   e) The absolute pride and ego.

This part of the mind is very hard to control; the key is not to force the change of habit, but to train it to submit to your will and it will be your slave instead of you getting slaved by it. The successful training of this mind will bring about the discipline in many things. Discipline in the martial arts (karate, kunk fu, tai chi, and many more) will bring about the physical self control of one's movements in self defense and the control of one's fear; while meditation can discipline one's anger; fasting can produce the control over hunger, but more of that later.

To achieve these kinds of high level of tolerance and patience, one must put forth the will to accomplish these goals in his mind first and then manifest it into reality; you must advance little by little in the building block of your discipline to be stable and lasting. Then you must test yourself over and over till you have mastered whatever you are working on. Here I will present some examples that I have attempted and succeeded in doing along my journey, and they are just to show the steps nothing more; each of us must develop his own curve of learning experience, and my examples will showcase the base line for yourself to see what you can do to improve and in these examples we will find steps that was taken by me to achieve my goals.

A. Fasting:

Fasting is the process in which you attempt to not eat any food for the duration of a selected time. I attempted to fast (water is ok, as well as tea or coffee" limited", as long as no sugar and no salt or any other additives added to the mix) for at least 12 hours; after I was capable of handling that, then I attempted 12.5 hours and so on and so forth till I achieved the desired fasting time of 20 hours or more with no food. This way I achieved my goal with a short period of time, and as I practiced my patience and tolerance to no food increased dramatically.

B. Physical desires:

Physical contact is the need of physical touch and the desire of physical temptations of the body. I attempted no physical contact for 3 days; then I took a break and then after a week tried 4 days with no physical contact then I took a break, and then the week after I tried 5 days and so on and so forth; when I achieved 10th day of tolerance of no physical contact, it became easier not to think of physical desires as an object, and it lost its thrall over me. I cannot say that I am completely over physical desires, but I can say that I am no longer its hostage.

Any kind of discipline you want to achieve is within your grasp as long as you are willing to do the work. There are a lot of disciplines out there, but these I have attempted and achieved my goals with them so I will suffice in mentioning these 2 only.

The mastering of this mind layer is one of the biggest leaps forward that you will take in your early development of your spiritual degree and advancing to the next level; achieving such a state will definitely put you on the right track towards higher spiritual awareness to achieve the degree of the man of wisdom.

4. **The conscious mind:**

It's the part of the mind that we operate in when we are awake. All day to day tasks is done here and also most of the learning is done here as well. Your daily job no matter how complex or easy it is, when you cook your meals, your social encounters, and all that you do when you are up and about is done here. This is the part of the mind that is like a UI "user interface"

a) This is where you feel every event and every encounter.
b) This is where you observe all that is in you and around you.
c) This is where you control fear and discipline yourself.
d) This is where you become the man of wisdom.
e) This is where you grow in every aspect of any matter.
f) This is where you unlock your subconscious to become enlightened.
g) This is where you learn and gain all the knowledge.

When you train to become a kung fu master, you will train the conscious mind, but your animal self will change its essence to become familiar with the kung fu discipline, but in your conscious mind you will have access to your animal self (kung fu discipline included) all decision are made consciously.

When you dream, your dreams happen in the subconscious part of your mind, but you will only remember your dreams in the conscious wake state and most of the time you won't remember. When you can explain and know your dreams and what your subconscious is trying to tell you, you become conscious and succeed in understanding the subconscious; your subconscious becomes your conscious even for the instant of that dream. The subconscious does not speak English and can only communicate through symbols as pointed out earlier; to understand these symbols you just have to go one degree deeper into the mind.

When you get angry you don't bring out the animalistic self, but your animalistic self becomes your conscious state if you are not in control.

The conscious mind layer operates on all the layers of the mind as the user interface, and it is the up bringer of the mind on every level.

The essence of being conscious is to operate all the layers of your mind in the conscious state, but at the same time the conscious must be in the control seat not any other layer. So consciousness is to break the layers of the mind and operate as one consciously.

5. **The ether cord:**

It is the back bone of the mind; it connects all the layers together and connects the whole mind to the cosmic mind. When we fall asleep the subconscious never sleeps, but it rises through the ether cord like an antenna to catch the informational traffic of the ether.

The OBE (out of body experience) comes in many different types, and one of these types is that the conscious mind will rise itself through the ether cord and travel through the ether side of things. The mastering of this ability will bring forth the experience of the ether world exploration, and access to the "Akashic" records. When experiencing OBE you have to be very careful not to cut the cord, because it acts as your anchor and life line to your body; if it is disconnected you will die please advance in this field and experience at most carefulness and in baby steps there is no rush.

The dream of revelations is only possible when the subconscious of the individual travels to that side of ether level of information, and bring back the required info without disrupting the flow. The person seeing the revelations must have certain aspects of them self as a saint or a holly man with a purpose and divine attributes. The man that is destined to see divinations is a seer chosen by the stars.

Note: The akachic records is the record of the whole universe and everything that happens in it on every level with everyone and it is in the cosmic mind recording the events.

6. The ether mind:

This layer is purely the higher self. It is where your guides and angels communicate with you and give you instructions. This part of your mind is the highest level of the human mind, and it has all the info of past life lessons.

To have access to this layer of the mind is done through these methods:

a) Hypnosis: to only be performed by a professional that is knowledgeable of the subject and is trust worthy to you personally.
b) Self hypnosis: to be performed by you; by making pre records with your own voice and record the

whole session; make sure you are confident to perform such an experiment and doing research on yourself; like your zodiac knowing exactly how you are before conducting this experiment. This is very important in order for you to do it right, without hurting yourself.

c) Intense meditation: performing a specific meditation and becoming deeply entranced.

d) Dreams: dreams are sometimes used to access these parts of your mind. Your guides and angels come into your dreams to spark a reminder of what you need to do or to warn you of a certain thing or just to guide you in the general right direction and the best of them all, is to give motivation to make you stronger and patient of whatever you are enduring.

e) Death: this part of the mind is looking for explanations and solutions for the next life experience. This part works with your guides to determine exactly where you need to go in your next life to advance spiritually and finish your karmas.

In this mind the spiritual senses are multiplied by a thousand folds; you will only notice this mind in the deep access states of the above situations; if not experienced in meditation you will go your whole life not knowing what these states of mind are, or how to recognize and interact with your guides and angels. When you recognize this layer and experiment with the above it will give you an upper hand of what is that you are doing in this life time and how to accomplish them.

7. **The human mind external** is the layer of the mind that consists of three parts:

The 1st part of the external human mind is the most outer shell of us and it determines the following:

    a) What others think of you.
    b) Gets confused with the conscious layer of the mind.
    c) Constantly changes with our experience.
    d) Here takes the role of culture and the way of living through our social convention of our society or the environment you live in and grew up with.
    e) Cultural religious behavior that have been passed down from parents and family.

The 2nd part of the external human mind is the reflection of your inner shining outwardly. It consists of the following:

    a) It's the like the skin.
    b) What you want of others think of you.
    c) Presentation of the self.
    d) Set by the needs around you.

The 3rd part of the external human mind presents others thought of you. It's like the part of your mind that interacts with the others outer mind, and it consists of the following:

    a) You exist when others think of you.
    b) People can influence your thoughts and behavior just by being around you. This is your personality behavior discord.

c) Stability of your existing mind through all the thought around you. You occupy that space at that time and your reality.

This layer of the mind may present some problems for you, because it can drive your ego and feed your fear. This layer if not protected can lead to a lot of dysfunctions in the entire mind, but don't worry unless you undergo mind control experiments or extreme harsh treatment you will be protected automatically by your mind's internal defense magnesium. Nothing can influence you unless you let them in on your own accord and will. That said, to affect these outer layers of the mind is to consciously discipline your entire structure of your thinking. The way you build your pyramid of thought is the way you will comprehend the world around you and how you interact with it and deal with everything that is in it.

Conclusion

The mind is very powerful and very hard to control; controlling the mind is like trying to direct a hurricane; when calm the mind becomes a gentle leaf.

All these parts of the mind tend to work together to understand who we are in this universe as humans. Any part of the mind that is not working properly will have dire consequences; a broken mind is extremely hard to fix; that said, there are some things that tend to lock us out of the full potential of our mind which is out of our hands; take pain for instance, pain can block your mind and hinder you physically and mentally (that is why torture is used in persuasion to change some one's MIND); the brain acts like a conduit for the mind and when the brain is busy with pain it cannot listen to the mind or have the will over it (unless you have the ability to suppress the pain and not hinder your will). When you calm your brain through meditation for example your mind can come through and your "will" will be free.

We have been given a great gift called the body; within this body we have the greatest tool which is the brain, with this body we got a great opportunity to achieve the light. Taking care of the body will give you the opportunity to master your mind and in doing so you will master your will.

Following your desires will destroy your mind and your animalistic self will control every aspect of your life, and this will bring about the animalistic state of desire of worldly stuff and you will be driven by ignorance.

"He who mastered his will, would have submitted his self, and he that willed himself, will have conquered the universe".

Emotions

Introduction

After the explanation of thought, exploration continues as the different aspects of spirituality unfold their true nature; in this chapter we have arrived at the next level that will bring us closer to becoming the man of wisdom which is emotions.

What are emotions? What makes us feel good, sad, or satisfied? What makes us feel frustrated to the point of giving up or gives us the courage to battle through the thickest of hardships? What makes us feel emotions and what drives them to make us do good things or fall into acts of evil?

To understand emotions we have to define emotions on its own level, but to do that we have to look outside the box for a meaning that can describe feelings or emotions; words fail to describe what a feeling is.

The subject of emotion allured a lot of people since the dawn of time; many philosophers and theosophists agree that to understand the mystery of spirituality is dependent on the explanation of such esoteric things through the experimentation and the living of these esoteric notions and experiences; this is also true in the matters of the heart. When often asked how do you feel? You can only explain a feeling that you went through; most people understand feelings by labeling them in such a way that any one that speaks your language can understand that labeled feeling. The universally acquired terms for feelings will bring the experienced feelings that we all go through from day to day, but to explain sadness to someone who is always happy is close to impossible, but if he experienced sadness he will know exactly what it means to be sad. Building on that note, a feeling is the state of the heart recognized by the mind in an event taking place at that time.

Emotions

Emotions are not the essence of an object, but how anyone come to form an internal opinion about the object (object here can be anything, anyone or any subject manor). For each observer, the emotions could be different for the same object of observation; each emotion is generated by the person observing that particular object.

As the mind can produce different frequencies through the objective of the brain, the same happen here with emotions; emotions produce different frequencies and run through the heart so to speak, but not the physical heart it's more in the gut area that we feel our deepest emotions.

Emotions will impose to ever change the mind and try to submit it, but the mind has to impose his will to submit emotions under his control or he will be slaved by the emotions; to be driven by emotions makes you blind to the reality of things it is the understanding of the mind with the heart for the combination of both will bring out the man of wisdom.

What connects us with our feelings?

Our feelings come from many encounters and for these encounters to take place we must interact with the realms through a conduit which are the senses. You can observe the physical world through the physical senses, and you will observe the spiritual world through the other part of the senses which are the spiritual senses. The interactions which will shape the world of the physical or the spiritual will only become enhanced through the training of the mind to intently intake the information while in a calm conscious state; the more conscious you become the more you observe. The mind will analyze and put forth this information for us where we can make sense of it; our emotions will put forth our opinion about the information that is collected. Between the two (mind and heart) we will make a final decision of the accumulated encounter of an event.

The senses are like the tools that the mind uses for the heart to feel while the mind understands.

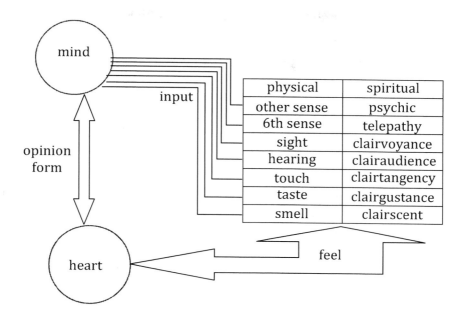

physical	spiritual
other sense	psychic
6th sense	telepathy
sight	clairvoyance
hearing	clairaudience
touch	clairtangency
taste	clairgustance
smell	clairscent

The development of the senses is our journey to understand the outside and inside world of our entire existence; otherwise nothing would make sense to the mind if there is no info about the observable object; how can the mind form an opinion about the matter if he has no input of what it is? Our conscious mind must see, smell, hear and touch to understand while the heart must feel these inputs to form the connection between the mind and subject.

The senses

I will divide the senses into two parts, one will contain the physical senses and right after that is the spiritual senses and they are as follows:

1. **Smell and taste:**

   Smelling and tasting work in similar way; half what you eat you smell, and half what you smell you also taste. What is smell but the aroma of particles travelling to reach your nose; then picked up by specific sensors that send the information collected to the brain; here it will be analyzed and identified where it is possible through memory.

   Smelling a perfume that wets the heart with warmth and ecstasy will bring out the sense of wanting of desires; these emotions fortify and satisfy the pleasures of the good things in life. Being in nature is one of the best natural aromas in existence, like the fresh rain smell in the beginning of spring. Since you always need to breathe to stay alive, and you don't have much choice it is better to be where you smell things of nature, because that will satisfy you down to the core. Tasting is like smelling it holds the key of sustenance for staying alive and enjoyment of the true fruit of life.

   Clair-scent:

   Clair-scent is the ability to intake the energy of PRANA in the act of breathing normal air and sustaining life itself, and at the same time to breathe in all the energies that are around you and fortify yourself to every limb and organ of your entire physical and spiritual body. These with Clair-scent sensitivity have the ability to sense energies with all its properties and intensity, and these people are good healers. Rekii healers are one of these sensitive Clair-scents where they can develop their skills through the training of their energy control through their sense, and they will be able to bring PRANA to the others that they are healing and themselves too.

Note: PRANA is a Sanskrit term for breath of life energy with all its forms and kinds.

2. **Touch:**

What is touch but the sensation of the physical contact of the outside world and you; your body picks up all kinds of information around you from any environment you are in; from hot to cold, dry, wet etc... this sense gives the grasp of the space that something occupies; it also gives the sense direction of things and their representation in nature. All these sensors on the body will help the brain achieve the certain sense of reality and existence in this world. Your mind will try to explain the relation between you and that object you're touching.

Clair-tangency:

This is the ability to sense all that occupies your domain and space; these people are good at sensing abnormalities and things out of place. They are good Reiki healers on the count of the scanning involved in Reiki; these people are good at sensing people's duress and tangible to all sorts of feelings they pick from others. They are sensitive to other worldly things and they are very good cleansers if they developed the gift.

3. **Hearing:**

What is a word, but a sound! What is sound, but a vibration! The right vibration will make the right noise; in which the noise will be deciphered by the brain, and then the heart's emotions will come into play governed by the mind. Hearing a poem or a beautiful rhythmic music might flutter your heart, and hearing an insult or a tragedy might break your heart. The right battle cry can give courage, and a certain screech can destroy your will from fear. Whoever can govern his conscious mind; will be able to steel his will and control all his emotions no matter how loud the chatter becomes.

Clairaudience:

Clairaudience is the ability to hear clearly the world of the spiritual chatter. To intuitively hear the spirits talking and make sense of what they say is a clairaudient. Clairaudients make great mediums they are good communicators through the non physical. This ability is different than telepathy because it's not mind to mind it is beyond audible chatter. For example the dog can hear way better than we do so they have higher clairaudience than normal people, but no mind to explain the phenomena (as we discussed in chapter one).

4. **Sight:**
What is seeing, but the observation of reflected light off objects! When you look at a yellow ball, the light reflects off the ball to enter your eye, then your brain analyzes millions of pixels to reanimate the information you just saw. We just can't understand all the information that we come by daily; the brain always discards garbage info unless guided by the mind to do otherwise. There is a scientific development in neurological research confirms the existence of empathetic mirror in the neurons.

The break through discusses that "when we experience an emotion or perform an action, specific neurons fire or activate, but when we observe someone else performing this action or when we imagine it, many of the same neurons will fire again, as if we are the person performing this action ourselves." What we understand from this breakthrough; if you see someone dancing, your brain's empathy neurons that are involved in performing this dance will fire; even you're just watching the act as it unfolds in front of your eyes. If you see someone getting stabbed or any other Haynes act of aggression the same thing happens; that is why the TV is the greatest mass mind control device so far. With the targeted adds and the acknowledgment of the human behavior and preferences from one person to another, will bring about the human mind down and to its simple form of engagement which is listening and watching; we all use the same basic principle and that's how targeted adds are used predicting the behavior of the human mind, and then target them with the right adds to right person. You see now how your eye is a very important key to a lot of observations, a picture is worth a thousand words that's how much complexity of a picture than just simple words; controlling what we see is very important to our keen improvement into our human psyche and becoming the man of wisdom. Watching porn can have such a bad effect on your healthy sexual life, especially on the behavior of the mind with such encounter. You choose what to watch and you control your mind to know the right from wrong go to nature and to the wilderness look at the sky and see how marvelous the universe can be, let your sight take you to the farthest mountain and see the most beautiful flower and become this humble observer we all seek to be.

Clairvoyance:

It is the ability to visualize anything in your mind with the sense that the thing you just visualized existing, but it is very important to implement the visualization of the effect and not the creation of an object. Clairvoyance is used in many spiritual aspects like OBE (out of body experience), this is one of the abilities that makes someone sight travel a vast distance and see what is in that spo, remotely far from the object. Clairvoyant people are able to find missing things on the real time continuum no matter how far or how well hidden the object is. It is seeing of the beyond without the use of the physical eye but the mind's eye.

5. **The 6th sense:**

The sense that we are going to talk about now is what we call the sixth sense it got its name since we couldn't link it to a physical sensation. Instinct drives this emotion, this urge, this bugging of the mind, this gut feeling, this voice inside you from you that tells when you are in danger or when you are right about someone or something; it does not have any physical senses of the sensory organ per se, but it runs deep in all of us. It gives us the feeling of the unknown and predictability of the incoming; all that comes in a form of feeling that we don't understand but it's there flashing flags at us. This sixth sense occupies the unconscious part of our mind that is why it is very unclear and much is unknown about it. We all have this sense, but some people are attuned with it more than others. Others are unaware of this gut feeling or they choose not to give it the attention that is necessary for the development of such a sense; in this sense the 6th sense is asleep within them they don't hear it any more, seldom to come out.

To explain when you are feeling the 6th sense is when:
a) Something is wrong and out of place or not right.
b) Getting the shivers or hair stand up without any apparent reason for it to happen.
c) When you see something you think you have seen before "DE JA VIEW".

d) Our blood runs cold to such an out worldly reason or illogical one.
e) A tinkle that runs from the top of our neck all the way down our spine.

This feeling is the 6th sense without us knowing that we have, yet we cannot explain this sense of incoming. To improve such a sense it requires the manipulation of the breath in a trance way; by clearing the unclear with every thought and every step you take. This could be hard at the start, but it will become second nature after you have been implementing this practice for a while you will be more attuned to the sixth sense and all its advantages. The advantage of this discipline you become a hardened thinker, multitask on the highest level (like you are only limited by you physical structure nothing else), focused on everything that is around you, clarity of all that is happening, and most of all intuitive on the level of anticipation.

Telepathy:

It is the ability to communicate with your higher self in order to accumulate any kind of information from the spiritual grid. Telepathic people can be angel communicators, tarot card readers, tea and coffee cub readers, and also people readers of all sorts; divination craft in all its sections of astrology.

The thing about telepathy is that it can predict the future, but the future is always changing so the prediction at that moment is useless. Only the reading of the stars can tell you a climbs of the incoming destiny, but not the future (destiny and future are two different things, destiny will happen in the future, but the future is never guaranteed it is always changing intermittent with other entanglement of the endless web of possible outcomes). The real purpose of telepathy is to establish the communication to your higher self and with the cosmic mind; this will make the access to the Akashic records much easier and retrieving information from that well of knowledge much quicker; it becomes your intuition to retrieve info and not your personal you. In the highest level of telepathy you become your higher self (unconscious mind) and in that state you can unlock 100% of your mind and the brain will follow and you become the complete man of wisdom.

6. **Other senses:**

There have been mentions in a few books that there are more senses than we already know. We only know the 6th sense that it exists and beyond that the science won't go any further, there is no evidence to support this claim. I will only mention that there are other senses that are beyond us at the moment for the lack of knowledge to know but they might exist. Maybe these sense unlock after we activate the rest of our chromosomes that are inactive, maybe they are sensory to know when disease come to our body, maybe it is seeing everything the way it is not the way it appears, and maybe all the regular senses become super senses all together. Speculating about this subject can go for ever, but I only wanted to mention it to have an idea of the possibilities that this presents.

Psychic:

It is the ability to have mind over matter in all its forms. The mental aptitude of the mind must be completely unlocked. The psychic ability must have the mind already in that state of complete mental freedom to be unlocked. There are degrees of mental power that can be achieved and there is some that you already have been born with, the cup can only hold its shape in liquid, so the bigger your cup the bigger you're well of mental capacity will be.

When all these senses physical and spiritual work together they will create such a complex emotion in which it is very hard to understand without the mind; that is why we feel it while the mind understands it. Feeling is the most complex of thoughts that our brain recognize and in order to understand the world around we must go through the comprehensiveness of the mind.

The Way of the Mind and the Emotional Discipline

Our spiritual journey must begin with our own self knowing, and to know our self we must explore and manifest as much experience as we can fit through the life span that we have. Learning will only move you forward and change your understanding of the world and beyond, but to truly explore your self is to think even how you think, and to see your mind at work in every aspect it is in.

Dealing with people is one of the experiences you will encounter, and knowing how to deal with them in every situation is a true success of the man of wisdom. Every situation you encounter will have a certain treatment you have to implement; understanding these different situations will grant you the true essence of wisdom, but you have to remember to not judge anyone; you can always help, but with no opinionated criticism. Unless you are perfect you cannot pass along your judgment unless you are absolutely perfect, and no one is perfect and the man of wisdom knows this in his heart. Everyone have to walk their path and no two paths are alike.

You have to think about people as they are your brothers and sisters, but on different paths; learn from them and help whoever is in need. We must Respect them and their paths, each has a level which is different than yours and that has to be taken into consideration; how much a person knows is very important, and it is up to the man of wisdom to indulge how much needed to help any person; if you try to get someone to over step more than they can handle they will fall hard; even help needs to be measured correctly for it to be helpful.

Exploring yourself and dealing with everyone around will enable you see who you really are and how you are according to others (not materialistically but socially and behaviorally), when you can determine the scale of people you will be able to weigh yourself and see what you need to improve. No one is perfect like we mentioned above, but each man would have at least one good trait, and if you implement the good traits and discard the bad ones from 50 men let us say, you will become better than these 50 men combined; nothing is impossible as long as you are trying to improve, even in baby steps you will still get there.

Exploring yourself must start in exploring your wounds, specially the oldest and deepest ones that have been pushed aside for so long, because you didn't know how to deal with them at that time. These old wounds tend to drag you down and hold you in the lowest state of your mind until you become that sorrow and sadness and you cannot think beyond that point of hurt anymore; you cannot think of anything else but why this happened to you, and how they wronged you.

We need to pass these wounds and heal ourselves and try to learn from them, and healing these wounds must be our 1st priority. For our spiritual journey to begin we must be able to be strong enough to have at least a little will. If you cannot fix yourself, how do you expect to fix anything out in the real world?

The question here is how do I heal these wounds?

If someone wronged you, you must forgive them and if you can't then you have to forget them there is no sense of remembering them; they will only raise your anger. Surpassing such a feeling or this mind state will require the strength of your heart and the resolve of your mind.

If a trauma of a childhood abuse has occurred, then the emotional distress will hinder the mind and put it in a terrible dark place. In this case you have to seek help in overcoming this state of mind or consequences will be dire. Past life regression might help in this state and having the right loving people around will definitely help.

Living with these wounds might be hard, and if you can't heal completely it is ok; a lot of people are still in this state of despair and that does not mean they you cannot advance; this hurting can make some people advance more quickly it gives them a reason to go on even harder; these are mentally strong people and self dependent; where others may be stuck until someone snatch them up from the hole of mental illusion, these people are mentally and emotionally weak or their experience was more than they can bare.

There is going to be a lot of knots in your life; the purpose of these knots is to make us gain the knowledge of life's lesson and to finish the karma we have accumulated. Our determination to solve these knots and make them strength towards our betterment rather than crippling our advance should be a priority that can be achieved through our minds will. You can achieve this goal if you don't dwell on these hardships; learn what we must and move on. The faster you pass these hardships the stronger your mind becomes, and the more you renew and heal yourself; you become stronger with every event never stuck always moving forward tackling one event at a time.

These knots will provide mental advancement in such a way it's like body building, but for your mind. These events become more potent while you advance higher on the spiritual ladder of mental capacity; this will only make you stronger and advance you even higher as long as you are capable.

Healing your mentality will produce a healthy and clear thinking of everything around you, and knots become tasks that you will conquer. When your mind set reach this point you become mentally and spiritually ready to take the bigger leaps into awakening the man of wisdom in you.

Understanding your emotions and how they work will move you forward towards higher spiritual understanding and living in a higher state of mind and advanced thinking. Some of us got bullied, some lost loved ones, some are ill, and so many more examples that come from every life out there; nothing comes easy, but always comes with a purpose.

Emotional dealings

Dealing with people is not an easy task, but in order to help anyone you must understand them while they are in that emotional state; you have to feel exactly what that person is feeling; you have to become that person in that moment of that feeling with all the facts intact, when you are capable of such an act you will be able to help, otherwise you will make it worse unless you are comforting that person in distress.

Always remember that you are always dealing with a mind affected by an emotional imprisonment (there are rare cases of dealing with mind only no emotion) that is why you have to put yourself in their shoes and walk in it for a moment; if you do that you will never mistreat a person ever again in your entire existence, because you will know exactly how that person is feeling at that particular moment as if you see what they see and you smell what they smell and hear what they hear and feel what they feel (it is instant remote viewing of a person).

What is mercy but the forgiveness of a person towards another that wronged him. You have grown so much that you can forgive easily; how big of you to embrace what has happened to you and took in the experience that made you stronger instead of the heartache that bestowed you. Problems will frustrate you, flip you, hurt you, test your faith, and push you to the max of what you can handle; your part is to know them when they happen and learn from them, which will lead you to a better understanding of thy self and knowing it. When you know your purpose your life will be much easier and it will be filled with love and enjoyment instead of anger and hatred.

GOD is very merciful, he never gives you more than you can handle; never think that you're alone GOD is always with you and helping you with every struggle you have; GOD knows what you need to excel, and what tasks you need to make you better; anyhow GOD will help you if you ask, but the wise man knows that not GOD or anyone else can do you work for you, but they can help you understand it and succeed in it. Life is a school and no one can do the exams for you; if others kept doing your homework you will FAIL; it is your homework, your karma, your destiny, and your journey; you have to take them head on and conquer them then move on to the next quest and the next lesson, and rise higher and higher into your spiritual awareness where you will eventually rise to the degree of the man of wisdom.

When dealing with a situation that someone has wronged you; you have to take a deep breath and think of a calculated action and punish in a calm ethical way by making them understand how they wronged you in an effort to explain the actions that they took did you harm. This way you will gain their respect and their apology. This doesn't work with ignorant egoistic people, and the best thing to do is to ignore ignorant people, because they're in a low level of spirituality and they need to work on themselves; best thing is to not to associate yourself with these people because they will drag you down. When they want help they can ask for it.

Understanding people gives you the key to unlock the understanding of peace with everyone around you; of course just their simple top part of their mind (what they like and not like very basic stuff) is enough for you to deal with them in most good sense. Understanding how to read people will get you the best of every relationship that is around you; in doing so you will always be in the part of the light which people love, because you understand them and know them in some aspect. When someone feels that you care for them they will acknowledge you in many ways, because they feel your essence of goodness that you are one of them and you treat them truly in an important way of appreciation and respect.

Imagine yourself in anyone's situation, unless you visualize their situation you can't understand what they are going through, so never ever judge anyone's way of thinking; they have their path and you have yours. Never try to change someone's opinion that's their opinion; make sure you hear their opinion and respect their decision even if it's not true, maybe your opinion is wrong, and maybe they are not at the level of knowledge you are at. You have to let them grow on their own till they accept the truth in any form it may come.

Pay attention to your actions and feelings, always think; don't let your tongue think for you think logically check it in your heart and then let your mind control the tongue to do its job. Understand each situation and deal with it as required, with passion and commitment to act from the heart with logic at hand.

Forgiving is such a powerful healing emotion, when you forgive that means you have surpassed that emotion of feeling sorry for yourself or pity that you don't deserve what you have encountered. You are higher than that self importance, instead replace that self importance with self worth and climb the ladder of enlightenment, be humble and accept it as it comes; even though experiences sometimes are not pleasant , but if they are happening to you that means you are being tested and taught by them. Every day is an experience on its own and your ability to recognize and learn from these experiences is how you become the man of wisdom.

When we talk about love, we have to take a bow in respect to that most beautiful satisfying feeling that have inspired writers, it frustrated the wise men to understand it, and brought philosophy to its knees to describe it. Nations have risen and fallen because of it and some say that the universe moves that way, because of that ultimate supreme purpose of attraction of things to each other which we call LOVE. Love is very sacred and understanding it is one of the hardest things to grasp, but yet it is so easy to achieve when experiencing it and living it. At this state whatever I write about love I am going to fall short so I will suffice by stating that; love has many forms and kinds and levels, loving your wife or husband is different than loving your friends and loving your family is different than loving other people etc..., when you love you must exhibit the highest truth in all the kinds of love otherwise it will be tainted and fake.

You need love to have wisdom and you need all wisdom to understand love.

Conclusion

When I faced hardship in my life, it only made me stronger that I became the master of my mind. That took a lot of patience to overcome with all the emotional stress that I came under. I have developed the ability to control my emotions through the focus of my mind, don't get me wrong I still get mad and frustrated and down, but surely it take a lot longer and a lot worse things to get me to that state. It's like you are filling a cub of water and every drop is an experience and every experience became knowledge in its own right, and that knowledge became a philosophy of understanding of my life. I came along way with this journey and there is still a lot more to come, and every day that passes, I become stronger and more stable and more energy focused while learning how to become a better me, I cannot attain perfection but I always thrive to become as perfect as I can be.

What we conclude from emotions, is that all our emotions tells us about our view of our heart towards an observable object or subject, and it is in our essence to feel so we can experience firsthand what we are learning, and moving forward towards our ultimate goal "ascension". Emotions can be our liberators and can also be our down fall if the mind has been lead by the emotions. Emotions can affect your thought and your thought can affect your emotions; just like the yin yang symbolic meaning you have to have both in balance for you to have inner peace, your heart needs wisdom to light its way, and your mind needs your heart to feel the truth. When thought and emotion become one single thriving action towards perfection, you become the man of wisdom.

Who Am I

Introduction

After emotions and thought; now it is only appropriate that we begin our journey of healing our mind and heart to become better equipped for what is yet to come. This is the 1st step into a big world that has many doors to worlds beyond our imagination. The keys to these doors are your mind and heart, and that is why it is very important to know "you", and understand yourself and how you work. Discovering your ways of understanding things and understanding the way you think of these things; you will eventually realize what you are capable of and what limits you, what gives you strength and what hinders you; know the essence of who you really are.

Who are you?

Where do you stand in this mortal coil?

Is your existence important?

Our real purpose stems from what we can do where our strengths and abilities play a big role in fulfilling the purpose of our existence. Let us embark on this great journey and see where it might lead us and what might we learn from this great structure we call "I".

Structure

We are a microcosm living in a macrocosm. When you move your hand your brain gives the order to your muscles to move in a certain way you want it move. Therefore all your cells "limps, muscles, skin, blood, etc..." will work together to execute this motion; each part provides a purpose to make the function of the whole as a rhythm.

All your cells are connected to your brain and they communicate with each other to make this motion possible in the physical realm; this transference of thought into electric energy into kinetic energy happens all at once to complete one simple task.

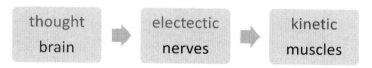

Each group of cells works as a cluster to be a muscle or a tissue or a nerve, but without the guidance of the brain all these limbs will become a piece of meat with no purpose; a severed hand will only hinder the capability of the body, but a damaged brain will kill the body; what we conclude is that all of these parts are important but the most important is the brain. The collective awareness of everything happening in the now is the key to self aware.

We have two sets of muscles; one being the regular muscles that we are in control of like the hands, and irregular muscles that we are not controlling like the heart where they serve their purpose without us knowing of it. The existence of the brain is to ensure the survival of the whole through all means necessary.

In every plant, animal, and human there is a DNA map for in which it defines exactly what is the shape, the abilities, and the existence of this entire entity. DNA is the information that all life forms rely on to exist; it will define the specimen in which what this entity will become. The existence will need every cell it has to form the shape, the kind and all the other things it needs, and every cell has the map; it is like a group of construction workers building a tower; you must have in the group the engineer to execute the plans, where the plans themselves are the DNA, the engineer is the life force (I will talk about in chapter 6) and the workers are the cells.

All this information is to tell you who you are from the molecular structure to the complete human being. To know who you are, you must know all the pieces that you are made of; if you want to succeed in becoming the man of wisdom with his entirety, the whole must exist through the mind and the mind need the entire whole to exist.

Who Am I?

As we now have an idea of what emotions are, and what effects they have on the mind; it's time to put them into action and our 1st action will be to figure out who we really are. We are all unique in our own way where no one is the same; you cannot define one person to be the whole, but one person can define an aspect of the whole. Each one of us has a unique way of thinking and a unique sense of things and how to view the world and how to understand it, and that will make you a very important aspect in bringing something to the table of existence.

The way you feel about a certain thing and your reaction to it will bring about your unique personality. There are about seven billion people on earth, and there are seven billion personalities not even one is exactly as anyone else. Some might be similar but there will be differences on deeper feelings and certain objectives even with twins.

Defining who you are can only be answered by one person, and that is you.

I am who I am, just the way I am. I am an observer of this world, a learner of the unknown, the walker of my own path, the opener of my future doors, and the decision maker in my own life.

My body and my brain are my tools to use where my mind is the cause, and my emotions are my motives.

Thinking with my heart, and feeling with my mind brings about the new understanding to this world. Keeping my body healthy is very important, because this is my tool that I will tackle this world and bring about new experiences. Every journey must start with a step in the right direction; that said our spiritual journey must begin from within ourselves exploring our own realm and understanding our own mind; while feeling every moment of every experience we go through, and that will define our understanding of our capabilities, which will earn us the knowledge of our self to the very fiber of our existence and how can we thrive and adept to every possible situation that is thrown our way.

There are many life times to cover, but at this time we have to master the self in this one "now". Past lives might help in a lot of cases, but we should not at this time dwell on past lives while we are still in the beginning point of spiritual advancement; when we are still struggling with the basic structure of our spiritual awakening we should take our journey one step at a time, and tackle this subject where it is less complex than the subject of our past lives. When we master our mind, at least grasping the identity of this life time, then we can go beyond into past lives. The now is very important, because it is the only part of time that actually exists the now is the action where it never stills; the future is coming every second and the past is already dead with every second.

In order to understand yourself you have to free your mind and your heart.

You free your mind by meditating, unhindered imagination, focused illustration, and open mindedness to new perception and learning of everything that is fathomable; at that time you see everything as it is, a small piece in making of the universe as a whole entity.

Your heart is free when the truth comes out; realizing the truth you become the real you and you will just BE. Break the box that was put there for you to limit you, and explore the new you; this box is shaped by other's thought toward you with the power of suggestion and the social acceptance, which tricked your mind into the box, but you and only you can break through and become free.

Discovering who you really are is not an easy task, and it could take a life time. You have to think of it as it comes, it is a long process it has started since your first words and will continue till your last breath. You reshape your understanding every time you get a new idea; then your mind and heart work together to make it fit with the rest of the building block of your understanding.

Exploring Your Abilities

Are you perfect? Well no one is, but you want to be as perfect as you can be; trying your hardest to become the best at what you are. like the old saying "be the best version of yourself".

Everyone has his or her own set of unique skills and attributes, which will make them who they are in the space that they occupy at this now of time; with the limited physicality that the laws of nature may allow. When you are looking for a job you would present your resume that include your strengths toward the job enlisted to be filled; same with the resume of your life, you strengths and attributes will be put into the right life that you are coming into; think of it this way whatever you meant to do here should show in your strengths and attributes; in conclusion you will be attracted to things of your interest that you are meant to do in this life time; if you're not happy with what you are doing as work that means that this job is not what you are meant to do in this life.

For example if you thrive in mathematics don't be a taxi driver; if you love driving don't go work as an accountant. What I mean here is that whatever you like doing you have to follow through, because that is your dream, and you have to realize that that dream will bring you joy and inner peace. I am not trying to belittle any job everyone is important as the next one, but it takes all of us to make the whole. When you know your passion you must follow it, because you will succeed in making yourself happy while giving 110% of a carrier, and not 50% of a job that you are there just to get paid nothing more nothing less. Sometimes circumstances force us into situations that we don't like or jobs we hate, but isn't this a part of the learning experience and the struggle to be free? Who will follow through and be what they want to be and not be in the prison of entangled struggle of the need.

Becoming happy in your daily life is the remedy for a fulfilling, peaceful, productive, thriving, and ever expanding mind. When you think bigger you will use your abilities not just for you but the entire whole, and the whole will thrive as well as you.

Acting upon the thoughts you create is a must; if you always talk about peace or anything in the matter of fact, and you never work upon it, peace will always be a distant future never attained and you will always be talking about it; when you act with peace not forcing the act but willing the act peace becomes your reality. Start with the self control and willing it to disciplinary submission, and teaching it to become more humble and peaceful through meditation and other means. At that point of an accomplished self peace comes in the now in its core essence living through you.

Everyone is very important and worthy to live in the here and now; everyone brings something to the table that is different always remember that no self is a waste otherwise it would not exist. No matter what you bring, these strengths or attributes are very important and need to be nurtured and practiced till mastered; these abilities that you hone or the mindset that you have is the gift in which you bring to this world.

What do you like doing in your life? A pilot, an astronaut, a taxi driver, a teacher, or an engineer...etc it is our desire to work in an environment that you love; this feeling is rooted deep inside of each and every one of us; like a diamond buried in the dirt, the more you search for it the more the diamond will clear up and show its shine. All this searching is for you to find your diamond. Your diamond is what you love to do in this life time; it is the secret to your happiness and essence of an excellent mind ever thriving for success in whatever you are here to do.

As the diamond is rough when it is found; same with your abilities they will be rough at first when you find out what they are; if you work and learn on developing your talents you will master them till these talents become second nature (a flawless diamond). For example a basket ball player must train every day so they wouldn't lose their edge same with every ability that you have or yet to discover.

There are a lot of things we don't know about ourselves, and the reason why we never search every aspect of our existence is because we always fall short on exploring our selves fully; one of these aspects is our astrological sign. When you were born, there was a certain planet that has been affecting your magnetic field and continuing to work for you and influence your every front. Imagine the waves at sea are caused by the moon and other planets gravity rivaling the earth's gravity; the ebb and flow of these interactive energies produce the mood of these great seas and oceans. These planets are millions of kilometers away and yet they still affect the state of the sea at that magnitude; now imagine what they are doing in the manor of man since we are made of 70 % water. These interactions of energies and their exchanges affect all living things from earth to other planets and to the smallest organisms that ever is in existence. For example on a full moon people act with animalistic nature towards each other more than any other day; go out on a full moon and see how people behave. The effect of planets on us is huge in many aspects according to ancient teachings; everyone's destiny is written in the stars since birth; this destiny of ours tends to help us in our quest to evolve spiritually and mentally. We make our choices but destiny writes the road with wakeup calls.

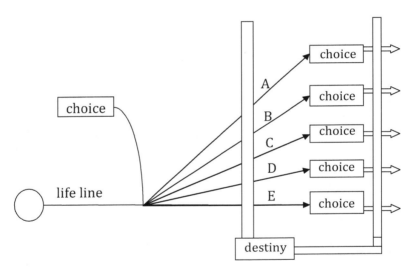

As we proceed on our life line, we have choices to pick from every situation we encounter whatever choice we make the act and the outcome is reflected by our reason. Whatever choice we pick (A,B,C,D, or E) there will be a reaction from an intertwined lines of possibilities that is so complex that no one can follow one road; it is always what you pick and choose that matters, everything else will just fall where it should. What we choose on the road can be defined by two categories good or evil, our judgment on our self should accomplish that no one else should; we have to pick the right from wrong even if the hard way is the right way. In this figure above, destiny will happen no matter what we choose and this "hit" of destiny could be anything it could be a near death experience, meeting your soul mate, winning the lotto, accidents, flashes of memory of a previous life, etc... what we choose to do with it after is what really makes the difference in our life. This wakeup call will have the jolt to set you on the right track, or the right push in the right direction for you to reach the next level of your conquest.

The options, opinions, and choices are yours to pick, but destiny will hit you like a bump (for awakening reasons); this bump could be anything, and after this bump you have more decisions to make and the web of decisions keeps going on and on and destiny thrives on every corner. Only the man of wisdom will understand his destiny and understand his purpose, and only the Creator can change any man's fate.

Astrology makes a big part of your life, and this effect of interchanging and mingling with everything around you will help you understand your spiritual journey. As the planets and other things affect you, you also affect everything around you. A real astrologer should be able to know even the day that he will die. Astrology is another world of spirituality and science all together and there is a lot more to this subject and straying off will only confuse the reader instead of helping.

A part of what you are, resides in the things you are able to do, your abilities come from different traits of life, some born with and others accumulated through knowledge and experiences; understanding these abilities will tell you a good portion of what you represent, and what you are here to do. The astrological aspect of you has the map of how things come to you, what attracts to you and what you repel; your destiny is sewn into the wool of the universe by the cosmic mind and governed by your astrological stars.

Purpose

All of us have a purpose, and this purpose is very clear to the person who is trying to attain wisdom. To know our purpose is to understand and know the essence of our core; when our purpose is known to us, life becomes easier and happier.

The question "why we are here?", has come up again and again with no definitive answer; and there is no definitive answer for this question, because each and every one of us has his own reason his own act his own refining to do. The faster you understand this concept the faster your journey begins. To attain such a quest and aim to get it, you must ask yourself one simple question "who am I?" Defining who you are come from the status of your mind that deals with the conscious and the subconscious; when you say I am "so" and "so" then you are dealing with the most social materialistic assigned name that brings you about your existence in a society. When you think you are the spirit that dwells in this life time of the body of "so" and "so" then in this case you have realized your true nature and this is the first step in becoming the man of wisdom.

To attain the man of wisdom status you must first know who you are and second find your purpose. Through your talents you will learn what your purpose is; your ability to do certain things brings about your uniqueness. Everyone must play their part in this grand play in this beautiful universe and everyone and everything is needed on some level somewhere.

If you have taken wisdom as your highest goal, your life will be full of the most effective heightened glorious way to become in perfect balance with yourself and the world around you, and this will bring about the true meaning and true life that we all wish to be in. After learning and experiencing what we need to experience and understand fully we will become enlightened.

If you choose ignorance in your life you would have wasted your time here, and you are bound to repeat this cycle over and over till you get through.

The Gift

The structure of the human body doesn't only depend on the parent's heredity, but also on the spiritual entanglement with the parents.

Each individual has free will of life choices and decision making of good and evil; all these choices must be made consciously and whatever happens in life is an event, but that event needs to be to be dealt with by the individual where the choices and decisions will determine what will the person be, no one is predestined to be good or evil you CHOOSE in being good or evil. You choose to help your neighbor, you choose to lie, you choose to kill, you choose to care for people, and you choose to be honest and make your living from the sweat of your brow. What you don't choose is how you die, where you die, what the destiny is holding for you when you're 30.

Don't be surprised with karma, always remember that we are here because we have a purpose to fulfill; fulfilling your karma is the reason for balance no matter what you did or didn't do, that is the reason why some are born with an illness and they are yet to make any mistakes, this karma has been dragged from a previous life, because it was not fulfilled. Karma brings about the balance no matter how bitter we would think it is, and remember that it could always be worse.

There are certain people, who are born with certain gifts or advantages, and every person has a certain advantage that comes with their package; this gift could be visible in this realm and could stay dormant till a change has occurred in the life of the subject. These gifts are unique to the personality of the subject that it is attached to; the earlier you realize and understand your gifts, the earlier you can harness your full potential to become the vessel of the great work, which will pull you forward towards success for yourself and humanity spiritually and mentally.

However you decide to use these gifts will define your mental stability, while karma is on the lookout for your intent and the good or the harm that you are doing. As so, some of these gifts have different degrees in what enrollment of life you will partake, the more you train the more powerful you become. I will mention a few examples of these gifts as follows:

a) Photographic memory: also called (eidetic memory), it is a gift that you (with extreme detail) recall any image from your memory even if seen for an instance.

b) Physicist: Albert Einstein's imagination saw the world in a different prospect of observation; most of his theories was imagined in his head then validated.

c) Philosophers: there is a good deal of great thinkers in the history of mankind that changed the course of thought around us. Aristotle, Pythagoras, Hermes Trismegistus, Confucius, Manly P. Hall, Allan Watt, The Dali lama, etc... they have discussed in detail the state of thought, and changed the history of humanity.

d) Sensitive people: there are some people that possess extra sensory perception that allow them to thrive in some fields, like people with great sense of smell and taste they becomes terrific chefs, so on and so forth. There is one type that we call a hyper sensitive that possess the ability to become a medium and spiritual naturalist, this type is extraordinary in thriving in the spiritual practices and helping others.

There are a lot of extraordinary gifts out there, and I think everyone has a gift that stays dormant till they unlock it. That said you should always cherish who you are and what you have and always be thankful.

The Belief System

In a part of discovering who you are, you have the systemic relation to your belief system that sets your character's way of thinking in to a structure; building your character changes every day and points directly at who you are.

To understand the belief system, I have divided it into the following parts:

a) The first category will deal with what have been pushed on to you since you were born. This belief system has been set for you by your parents, relatives and elders;

this form of belief is set by cultural acceptance and only following what you are told by the older faces of your society. This gives you the first stepping stone of your belief system, if you believe it as it is in your own mind it becomes your belief.

b) All of us go through life and we experience a lot of things, what you accumulate of thoughts on these experiences with life is your second stepping stone on to your belief system. This is your way of experiencing yourself and how you see the universe in your mind.

c) The accumulated knowledge from an external source. It is what we learn without the experience, only pure knowledge. Like books, movies, schools, etc...

d) The fourth category is the most important or the most successful, it is the combination of the previous all; it is the root believe since childhood with open mindedness into philosophical understanding of the working of all three categories into a working theory of a belief, and then into implementation and execution of the belief with ever changing into the best. It is the ideas that accumulated from experiences in your life over this period, and adding the books you have read and executing the thought of all that into one solid action in life, that's what we call a great belief system.

We make our own philosophy of life, our thoughts shape our life; we live it according to our own believe that is shaped by our own mind, and not following any one's else mind, but our own. We are on the righteous road to the light of becoming the man of wisdom.

Conclusion

You are not just who you are now, but you are a part of thousand you(s), from a very long ago still coming into formation with endless resolve of becoming the best that you can be, yet to come, but already on the way.

"Here Cometh the man of Wisdom"

The Creator

Who is the Creator

How can I bring a thought of the creator into this world, and GOD is all the thought and the manifestation of thought in all the worlds. We need to acknowledge that there is a higher force that is in control of the universe, with that thought we can move forward. What to know of GOD must purely be in the sensing of all that is; when you look around you could feel all the vibrations of everything that is around you, it's all alive.

Either GOD exists as a part of the world and GOD becomes the world, or GOD exist outside our reality looking down on it. To be on the safe side; GOD must exist in this reality and outside the boundaries of the physical and the spiritual worlds. Think of GOD as the back bone or the soul of the world where no physical body can be alive without a soul; if GOD is the soul of the world then our reality is just clay until the essence of GOD or the soul comes into this physical clay. Now we can say that GOD exists in the thought, while the soul is the extension of GOD; GOD is not physical anymore that is why you cannot see GOD. GOD's thought makes the physical world and GOD's soul makes the spiritual world, in the end GOD is the creator of both worlds.

When people try to contain GOD in a person or a vessel it seems that the concept of GOD is beyond them, because they are searching for evidence so they can believe. A belief does not come from seeing and touching and smelling, but it comes from the deepest wisdom of knowing in the mind and the heart; this matter of knowing must be on the pyramid's building blocks of faith embedded into the structure of understanding the whole. People that try to limit the creator "GOD" into specs or ideas that they can wrap around with their mind has a certain lack of believe to the real idea of GOD.

To think that life just happened out of nothing, seems to be a bit faithless in a sense of the lacking in to the understanding of the whole; the master piece that is us, set in the master piece of the universe must have an intelligent all knowing creator behind it, because things don't just happen.

Those who believe in the physical attributes of GOD have a mere dot of the creator; these attributes of GOD are only description of what GOD can do, and not even close to know the concept of GOD. These people have skipped their initiation of knowledge and have shaky feet in their faith of believing; this initiation is when you feel GOD's presence in everything that is around you. You cannot teach a belief if the person on the receiving end doesn't see it in their heart and feel it in their mind.

Explanation...

GOD is all around, like a web of light surging in everything and everyone, yet GOD is beyond the light.

GOD is like the atom that makes up all that is in the physical world, yet GOD is beyond the physical.

GOD is like the water that makes everything alive, yet GOD is beyond life and death.

GOD is the limitless soul that governs the universe(s) with the wisdom that the human mind cannot comprehend.

GOD is the law maker, yet GOD is above any law.

GOD is the alpha and the omega, nothing before GOD and nothing beyond GOD.

GOD is the singularity itself beyond the concept of male and female. GOD created the two forces that everything is made out of.

GOD dwells in everything, yet GOD is bigger than the universe(s).

GOD is the whole energy, all the energy.

GOD made the cosmic mind that governs the cog wheel of the universe.

Expectations...

GOD is not harsh, GOD wants you to understand and become better. The harder for you to learn and accept the harder the lessons become, and vice versa the more you know the easier the lessons become. But that doesn't mean the lessons will be easier, no they for sure become higher learning but the way to them becomes easier as we become higher on spiritual ladder.

The man of wisdom is the closest to GOD; he seeks and sees GOD in everything and everyone, and the man of wisdom understands a higher glimpse of GOD than the rest.

The man of wisdom has a purpose and his purpose in life is to understand everything he can understand; in doing so, the man of wisdom starts to understand the workings of GOD through all that is.

Levels of acceptance and expectations:

1. The highest purpose in life is perusing to be the man of wisdom; the wise with a heart of gold is the man that understands GOD in a way that every single task is driven to the higher understanding of universal purpose. This is the hardest road to complete, but it is the most satisfying and gratifying level of all. When knowledge is accumulated, the man of wisdom leaps forward in executing that knowledge and implementing it into all that he does.

2. Devotion is the shortest way to GOD; but very hard to apply from the heart. The complete surrender to the creator is to have the complete trust, love, devotion, and faith in GOD; when you completely achieve that state of devotion you would not exist here anymore, and you will be ascended. This is the way of the heart and love, you must have pure heart and that is the purpose of love. You don't graduate from love you become love.

3. The ones that follow the worldly things can ascend, but it will take them very long time to do so. This type of people live in fear of GOD not love (unfortunately that is how most of us are operating in this era, because we have lost the real purpose behind our existence, which is not the collection of worldly possessions, but to know the self in the search for ascension), they will advance ever so slow, depending on a guru or a teacher or a religious figure to help them (advice "please get all the help that you need from anyone, but NEVER follow a man"). Their way of ascension will come from the generosity that they bestow upon the other less fortunate people giving away worldly stuff which will balance their self in "the eye" of GOD. They try to do as much as they could without the understanding of the why. Their ignorant to some degree, but fearful of the outcome of their actions, and that will put forth the positive form of satisfaction of being good on some level.

4. Atheists are on the lowest degree of ignorance and stubbornness, they believe in nothing and that is a belief by itself. A true atheist is to believe to not have a belief. They cannot find a purpose for their life as if they existed accidentally for an instant in this universe of randomness and faded out into nothingness completely dead; little that they know that a spark of life will go for ever as long as there is an energy guider of this complicated essence of all that existed, existing and yet to come into existence. The ego on this level of people is bigger than their heart, mind, and spirit they are on one of the lowest levels of acceptance. Till they grow out of their ignorance and harness their minds and for love to enter their heart they cannot start their journey towards greatness. Just because they don't think that GOD exist makes it true, it's

just their opinion about a subject that is bigger than they can comprehend.

Conclusion

Finally I will say that faith in GOD is a feeling and an observation of everything around you and every thought from you is an action towards a reaction.

Having faith on your side is like having endless amount of resources.

GOD does not need you, but you are in need of him, for GOD to need you he will not be the Supreme Being, but for you to need GOD is to grow spiritually and mentally.

Let it be, take a deep breath, close your eyes and feel all that is around you... then just be.

The Soul

Introduction

Every spiritualist understands the importance of all spiritual aspects of his being. One of these aspects that are directly connected to our liberation is the soul. Trying to define the soul is like defining the essence of GOD; any word you try to use to describe the soul will fall short, but to understand the soul we must have a close enough concept we can relate to till we at least see the works of GOD in all.

The spark that is in every living thing defines the soul for what it is, but with loose ends. It is the light that shines from inside of every living thing but not seen, or proven. The soul is of the other science; the science of the spiritual wisdom, the science of GOD, the wisdom of the ages, and the initiation into the hidden knowledge.

Understanding the soul is like capturing light with your bare hands every time you get close it slips away; yet it is the essence that is impeded in everything that is in existence.

After an extensive research into the subject of the soul, I only got illusive answers from all external sources, nothing affirmative always something missing. After talking to elders and priests that are from various different religions, non have gave me a definitive answer or a convincing answer always broadened answers that are very general in nature. The theory of what the soul might be is out there, and for it to make sense to me I had to visualize it correctly. I believe that this is the truest illustration of the soul that I can comprehend at this time.

The Manifestation of the Soul

The soul has been defined in a lot of different ways; the words to comprehend the soul to what it really means has been misused and compromised. To nail the definition of the soul we have to split the soul into two parts these two parts none of which can exist within a body or a vessel without the other. These two parts are as follows:

1. The 1st part of the soul is called the soul ether; it is made by GOD and it is a part of GOD a shining light from GOD. It is the spark of all sparks it is the source of all, yet bound to the creator. The soul ether cannot be tamed, touched, controlled, sold, and corrupted or otherwise. The soul ether dose not participate in abilities, qualities, strengths, weaknesses, or personality in any way shape or form; it occupies only the power or the spark from GOD which is needed in all to all exist on the physical plain; it contains all the wisdom and all the love yet inaccessible. The soul ether is like a cell made out of light and GOD is the body in which that cell exists in amongst billions of others (this is just an example to bring the definition to a human level of understanding).

The soul ether belongs to GOD and GOD alone, we borrow it to exist here and upon death this soul ether returns to GOD.

The soul ether is always connected to the source through the ether currents that is in the spiritual realm while still connected to the body through the ether cord; in doing so, the soul ether will witness information from the spiritual realm while the subconscious sometime sees things in that realm; if the conscious as we discussed in the 1st chapter, can explain what the subconscious is presenting (same effect can be achieved in the deepest trance of meditation) then you would have access to information beyond this realm; information that could be premonitions of things that might happen (for example), or access to the teachings of your higher self, or even the cosmic mind... this information is available to everyone, but are you sensitive and pure enough to observe and know them?

Understanding the language of symbolism and all its attributes will grant you the access to the ether world through your subconscious. Understanding the ether will give you the understanding of the soul ether. We tend to put limits on our selves just to justify our laziness which won't help us in ascending or achieving any higher understanding of the esoteric laws, but to put this concept in plain symbol words; the soul is the essence of GOD and we cannot fathom it without becoming it.

2. The 2nd part of the soul is called the spirit or the core self (the self); this part of the soul is the base in which all your reincarnations are stored (like a memory stick); all

that you have accumulated over all your lifetimes is stored in the self; this memory is inaccessible in the conscious state of mind; when we die the memory of our conscious mind is dumped on to the self and wiped clean; that makes the self the real you over the period of your entire existence.

This knowledge is cloaked and hidden from the uninitiated into the mystical esoteric knowledge; the reason behind this is when there is a shaken foundation of knowledge the wrong idea or view will be swept into the mind, and that will be disastrous to the person of ignorant prospective on this subject; we must protect a lot of the information that is being presented here. So please keep an open mind and if you have reached this sentence in this book you are meant to be presented with this information. The cosmic mind works in mysterious ways and you are worthy of such information. The uninitiated are the ones that are stuck in ignorance and deception of worldly things, and they refuse to move up on the spiritual scale.

The core self is the one that sticks to more of the physical stuff; the learning through trails and life times of experiences and different scenarios of the happening and even repeating the same experiences because of ignorance, but eventually we will move on higher on the spiritual scale.

The purification of you will stem from your acts and intents pushing on the physical reality through the means of your consciousness.

The biggest secret of ascension is to awaken the self or the spirit and make it conscious, and to do that is to break the shell and become the soul ether. This is the ultimate union of complete enlightenment that every spiritualist seeks. The ultimate purpose in the life of a man of wisdom is to break the barrier between the soul ether and the spirit so they become one; that implies that you as the self will merge back into the great creator through the soul ether. That can be established with the following:

1) Meditation and discipline to purify the heart and mind.
2) Wisdom through knowledge and love.
3) Love everything that is from GOD.
4) Fasting and mantras to purify the self.
5) Absolute submission to the divine in whatever happens.
6) Knowing the self and finishing all of your karma.

"When the soul ether and the soul self become one, you will see all and all will see you"

The spirit or the self is a part of the non physical realm of the body which we call the subtle body. This field of energy we cannot see consists of the aura of the body which we will go over later in this work.

The spirit is different from the soul ether because the soul ether never changes, but the spirit is in constant state change to fit the ultimate purpose in uniting itself with the soul ether.

The most basic understanding we will imply here is to further the concept and bring it closer to the reader for further assimilation in order to further their involvement in the spiritual realm, and to push their mind into opening their imagination into bigger truths and slowly move into them.

The self is a part of the mind as we discussed in the first chapter; the experience that is accumulated in the self is manifested as a feeling as well as an acknowledgement of that state; if the spirit is not involved with these two parts then the self will never advance and will always have to start from zero upon every death. No more refining no more growth that will ever take place without the mind or the heart and the self will halt.

Your character has been building up for thousands of lifetimes refining and clearing its true colors. Life time by life time we accumulate all that we experience and put it into the spirit where it sets the scale for the self on the spiritual degree.

Note: when a spirit gets stuck here on the physical plain it becomes a form of a ghost. The feeling on the spiritual realm is multiplied by a thousand folds, and that is why when someone has dies a horrible death or injustice death by someone they loved or when revenge takes over the spirit's every fiber of the being, these spirits never accept death as inevitability. The mind is over matter, and when there is enough fuel (feelings multiplied by 1000) to ignite the fire in the spirit's heart it will give enough reason to the mind to do what it will and nothing can stop it until justification has occurred or helped by a medium to pass over and continue the journey. The spirit that stays here tries to stick around the same area that it died; at this point they will occupy a negative space and since there is no body to control they cannot touch anything but they try never the less, and they will appear as an anomaly.

Conclusion

What we know about the soul might not be much, but when we conceive a little bit of the truth about what the soul really represents you will become a little closer to understanding the truth and what you are meant to do here and why is this unique thing given by GOD to us mean so much. We must be thankful that we have been allowed this opportunity to grow where our spirits will get a little closer to our soul with every lifetime of goodness and positive prospective on understanding the whole; step by step we will unfold these layers of our self, till we find the purified core and the self will finally become the soul.

The Life Force

Introduction

We have defined the soul and its dwelling in everything that exists, yet there is a force that makes everything move and grow on the physical plain, and it is separate from the soul. This energy or life force is the mover of subtle bodies in everything that is alive.

This force exists on the spiritual plain and on the physical plain simultaneously, for it has effect on both. To say this more correctly all that exists on the physical plain has its mark or essence on the spiritual plain; the life force plays a role of bringing the connection between the physical and the spiritual.

All the physical matter is made of one substance one base which is the atom and all the atoms are the same structure. Here I ask, what is the life force that we are trying to define? Is there any signature for it in nature?

There are some particles that are smaller than the atom and they play a magnificent role in influencing and manipulating matter; this energy particle is called Tachyon (subatomic particles). Science discoveries are breaking through every day and we are learning of how these particles are behaving with matter.

What moves these particles? What are the unseen forces that tend to sprout life? How these forces play a role in the expanding of our physical existence?

The existence of all the vegetation in our realm have to come from somewhere; water and food is needed to ensure our survival where we turn these foods into energy so our body can survive.

The degree of substances

Everything that is in existence has a spiritual degree or a level on the ladder of spirituality. This tells us how pure is the substance to the divine or how far away from ascension it really is. This scale is very important and will provide the knowledge to understand the structure of the spiritual degree of things.

This information is to put a scale into our understanding of all things physical and where to start, and what to expect of these effects on the human being as a whole. What are these energies and forces that can envelope the physical as a structural block of nothingness, into a colossal creation of a beautiful manifestation from a pure intellect form that can operate on its own manually. We have to acknowledge the incredible work that goes into even sprouting one flower; how magnificent is the power that such creation can exist in the first place. Just how that is possible where all levels of creation is needed to even execute even the sprouting of this flower.

We need to define all these levels before we can even begin to understanding the working of the life force and they are as follows:

1. *The soul:* the untouchable spark from GOD.
2. *The mind:* here we emphasize the mind into the cosmic mind also known as the God head. He is the purist of all things. The cosmic mind is the highest after the soul ether, he is responsible for all creations limitations and order, because order must behold the universe or the universe will come into chaos. The correct way of things to happen and making sure they happen is the cosmic mind in action he is just under the infinite's roof as supreme communicator and thought dweller.
3. *The self:* It is the purpose of the existence or it gives matter its purpose. It provides the reason for the existence and puts things on the map of existence and how it performs the actions through karma. The self is the listener of the mind and it obeys his commands and abides by his laws. Without the self, things cannot appear here on the matter world and it wouldn't have the

purpose to exist. It is the 3rd level on the grand scale, and it is the cog wheel of the universal purpose.

4. *The cosmos*: the cosmos is the purest matter in terms of spirituality. The cosmos are all the anti matter and other elements yet to be discovered, this is star dust where stars are born and their forces control the matter on a grand scale that we cannot yet imagine; all these stars are beings in motion in this vast universe just like earth, these cosmos are the living honor of the closest thing to life, yet it holds the secrets to control destiny and effect on all matter.

5. *Fire*: the purist form of matter. In alchemical tradition it purifies all matter.

6. *Air*: this is what surrounds living things and give them the space they occupy in this world.

7. *Water*: the living essence of all things nothing can thrive without it. It occupies around 70% of anybody that is alive.

8. *Mineral*: it is the lowest on the ladder and yet as important as all; without it the mind cannot do its work, the self has no purpose, the cosmos have no control, fire has no start, air has no space, and water has nowhere to fall on.

9. *Tachyons*: they are the glue of the universe and it needs all of the above for it to have a purpose. It is the life force that makes up all the subtle bodies of all that is alive.

Beyond Matter

Our bodies are made of cells and these cells are made of atoms. These atoms consist of:

1. Protons (positive charge)
2. Neutrons (neutral charge)

3. Electrons (negative charge)

The magnetic field is what holds the atom together just like our solar system and most of the atom is made of empty space. If you empty the space of a group of atoms and put them side by side in a 1 cubic centimeter it will weigh about 100,000,000 tons. We are barely scratching the surface in knowing matter, but we have come a long way from ignorance and science is moving forward in vast leaps.

Tachyon energy:

Tachyon: according to Wikipedia "is a hypothetical particle that always moves faster than light. The word comes from the Greek meaning rapid. It was coined in 1967 by Gerald Feinberg.[1] The complementary particle types are called luxon (always moving at the speed of light) and bradyon (always moving slower than light), which both exist. The possibility of particles moving faster than light was first proposed by O. M. P. Bilaniuk, V. K. Deshpande, and E. C. G. Sudarshan in 1962, although the term they used for it was "meta-particle".

Most physicists think that faster-than-light particles cannot exist because they are not consistent with the known laws of physics. If such particles did exist, they could be used to build a tachyonic antitelephone and send signals faster than light, which (according to special relativity) would lead to violations of causality. Potentially consistent theories that allow faster-than-light particles include those that break Lorentz invariance, the symmetry underlying special relativity, so that the speed of light is not a barrier.

In the 1967 paper that coined the term, Feinberg proposed that tachyonic particles could be quanta of a quantum field with negative squared mass. However, it was soon realized that excitations of such imaginary mass fields do *not* in fact propagate faster than light, and instead represent an instability known as tachyon condensation. Nevertheless, negative squared mass fields are commonly referred to as "tachyons", and in fact have come to play an important role in modern physics.

Despite theoretical arguments against the existence of faster-than-light particles, experiments have been conducted to search for them. No compelling evidence for their existence has been found. In September 2011, it was reported that a tau neutrino had travelled faster than the speed of light in a major release by CERN; however, later updates from CERN on the OPERA project indicate that the faster-than-light readings were resultant from "a faulty element of the experiment's fiber optic timing system". "

At this point in our journey, the science discoveries of our age deals with subatomic particles and the knowledge about hypothetical theories of their movement and the existence of a behavioral structure of such particles; these advancements are just called something different in science but at some level they are the same esoteric knowledge that haven't been proven yet. Known by our ancient ancestors, we are rediscovering the hidden information of these essential particles which is getting us closer to answers to some of the metaphysical questions, like the chi energy manifestation.

I have searched and searched and tachyons seem to be one of these elements that can represent the chi energy or life energy. Since science can't proof its existence but aware of it, that only tells me one thing, tachyons are not for sure the particles of the life energy, but whatever this chi energy is it must be very similar to how tachyons are behaving. To approach this matter in another way let us assume that tachyons is the chi energy, until further notice, for the sake of understanding this subject of the subtle life force; we can say that tachyons are the energy that surrounds our physical body and make up our chakras. Tachyons exist everywhere at the same time, because they are faster than the speed of light, and faster than light they become outside the laws of time; what we conclude is that the tachyons can exist on the physical and the spiritual plain simultaneously since they are not bound to time.

The question here is what are the tachyons for us? How can we make them work for us on the spiritual level?

Since the life energy makes up our chakras, we can say that the tachyons are the ones that control our chakras, or who ever can control the tachyons can control their chakras. When we say mind over matter, it really means the structural building of the universe bends to the minds will, we conclude that the mind can be the biggest manipulator of these beautiful glowing energy orbs we call tachyons, can you see the potential that is lurking all around us?

When one of your chakra's tachyon energy is slowed down, an unbalance will happen and cause a disease. In theory, a dowser (Reiki healer) can manipulate these tachyons into balancing ones chakra and that (if not too much damage has occurred) will cure this disease, and bring about the balance on to the chakra.

Imagine all disease can be cured just by balancing your chakras and control the flow of tachyon energy; this is the art of mind over body.

In a perfect spiritual world disease should not exist. So to bring about such a world you must be conscious on the spiritual plain while you walk consciously on this physical plain. The man of wisdom knows exactly how this is done and this is not something you study or learn that is something you need to acquire and move into consciously.

Healing is not permitted or it will not take place until the person with the disease understands and accepts why this happened to them. Karma has to take its place and fulfill its purpose, because everything has a purpose and it won't be balanced if everyone just did wrong, and the unbalance will bring chaos and disturbance in to the reality of existence; like a circle which is in perfect balance, karma has to be the perfect circle. To understand the reality of your disease and accept it as a state of mind is our quest to health; then and only then healing can take place to ease pain and suffering, just like the doctor he has to understand what's wrong with you before he can give you the right meds that actually can help you otherwise he can kill you. The full heal will come when you understand your purpose with the disease that you have; what is the lesson from this and how do I learn from it? What is disease but the lack of something in your system that is out of balance?

There is no disease in a perfect being.

The life force in action

How does a seed become a plant, and what triggers the sprouting of these plants?

The life force exists everywhere and in everything that is alive, in the eastern traditions they call it "chi". When a plant is seated in the soil it stays as a solid until the right accommodations have been acquired; what we mean here is soil, water, air and finally heat or light must be accommodated for life to take place; if any of these requirements were not accomplished the seed will fail. To trigger this sudden burst of growth into the physical plain the chi has to come into play. What is happening here on the small scale is the raising of the vibration of the seed; water, earth, air, and light provide perfect conditions to sustain, but the vibration rising inside the seed from the life force will push forward the sprouting of the seed; the seed's single minded consciousness is triggered into action through the power of the chi moving into the seed's own DNA and triggering the map of length width, and the characteristics of the plant it is growing, and then the sprouting takes place into the physical world to become a full manifestation of whatever the living plant is.

In every plant, animal, human, or any other species there is a map which is called DNA. This DNA is embedded into every cell of the organism and it defines exactly what it is as the structure, the organs, or what is called "the set".

Steps of the seed growth:

1. Seed: no change, dry, but holds the map for the mother plant we call DNA.

2. Water and earth: sustain and condition the seed, environmental potential for coming into the physical.

3. Chi energy: raising the vibration and triggering the DNA into action, seed sprouting.

4. Sunlight and air: full manifestation, producing more seeds and ending a cycle.

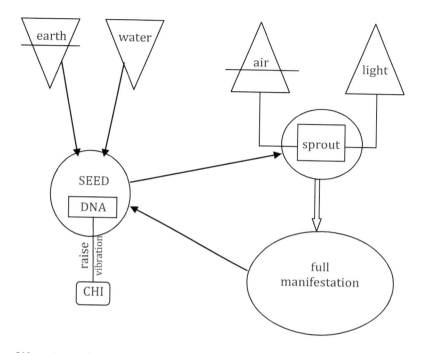

We give the plant world manifestation as an example, because the animal and the human manifestation are much more complicated. This example will touch the reader's mind and fully comprehend the role of the chi into the spiritual world and how to use it correctly.

When you meditate, the chi energy swirls and moves with in you and in order for you to use it you have to be able to sense it and drive into it in order for you to control where you want it to go. That is exactly what the monks have been doing since ancient times through their physical manifestation of the chi into action on their body they become super humans.

Conclusion

To exist on the physical plain you must have the chi well intact with in you, this chi is one of the most profound energies that the mind can manipulate and unlock its full potential. A real tai chi master can concentrate his chi to accomplish astonishing things here on the physical plain, which is impossible to do with the normal laws of physics.

Life goes on and on, and the chi is everywhere always swirling and moving, ebbing and flowing, coming and going, circling and traveling over and over. Nothing here is created only transferred, as long as you keep that in mind you would have accomplished a good step forward into the world of healing.

The chi could be used for good or for evil, but if a person uses it for evil it will come back at him at a terrible price and it will sling shot him down to the lowest realm of ignorance and material existence and the loss of some spiritual degrees. There is harmony on every single plain of existence and all must obey the balance, the man of wisdom only uses his power to do well for his betterment and the helping of others.

The Realms of Existence

Introduction

The spiritual realm is a term used to describe a plain that exists outside the boundaries of our physical realm. For example, the mathematicians try to define the term infinity by using a symbol to make their life easier; the term infinity"∞"cannot be defined in a normal state, because infinity is beyond the imagination of any mathematician, but we must use a variable representation of that which is beyond our understanding in order to solve mathematical problems. The same thing is when we use the term "spiritual" the use of this term is to make our understanding of this subject matter much easier and maneuverable for usage in that which we cannot define, but we must bring it to a symbolic term in order to use such valuable information to solve mysteries beyond the physical realm, and give an explanation for supernatural events.

When we talk about realms, the idea of a place or a kingdom comes to our minds and here it is exactly what I am pushing through as a thought. The idea of having a whole place that is as vast as the physical realm and occupy a space in the "where" it is residing.

Our naked eyes can observe most of the physical matter, but there are some realms that our eyes lack the requirements to see. The things we see here on the physical plain have its exact image on the spiritual plain, but on the spiritual plain they exist as a different combination of elements that is not of the physical.

To conceive such realms we must think outside the box and move with our imagination to weave an image of such a place existing. A deep meditative state or a trance will allow the user to see such worlds not only as an image but a real manifestation of mysterious objects that floats outside our realm.

Deeper and deeper the rabbit hole goes and the realms of existence keep unfolding layer by layer.

The Connections

The spiritual plain is a web of connections that connects everything on the physical plain with its original existence on the spiritual plain; intertwined together, the spiritual and the physical are within the unseen connections that reverberates through all that exists. Everything impacts its surrounding at some degree on the physical plain where the spiritual plain can impact all that is beneath it.

Come to think of it, the spiritual plain is the invisible spinal cord that holds the life force within; the act of the spiritual will tune the shape of the physical; in other words all that happens on the physical must happen first on the spiritual and then it moves to the physical.

This notion of the spiritual gave me the perfect conclusion to the theory of "Déjà vu"; a Déjà vu occurs when the subconscious mind takes a sneak peak out of your mind into an event that is taking place on the spiritual realm; in that brief moment your conscious mind gets a glimpse of that image from the subconscious mind. The conscious mind has already registered that something you had already seen on the spiritual by your subconscious. Since the event occurred on the spiritual and that exact event got embedded in the subconscious and the fact that your conscious picked up on this message from your subconscious as it is happening on the physical, therefore déjà vu becomes a mind puzzle between the subconscious and the conscious to know what is real. Clearly the event took place on the spiritual then moved to be executed on the physical and your subconscious was the witness, and for that one brief second you were foretelling the future in your conscious state as the event unfold.

Before we indulge into the spiritual realm we must discuss the existence of things that is on the physical realm, because to understand the spiritual we need to understand what it really influences.

The effect of the spiritual upon the physical is very rapid and spontaneous, which makes our mind have its essence half dipped into the spiritual realm as a constant state. The subconscious is in the spiritual realm and the conscious is always in the physical; when you become conscious even of the subconscious your will becomes powerful enough to influence the spiritual realm, and in doing so you can influence the physical through the spiritual, and that is how miracles are performed and pushed through to our physical reality.

Physical Manifestations

Atoms are in a constant state of vibration; we know matter more specific as a substance from the number of protons, neutrons and electrons that is impeded in every atom. Furthermore the heavier the atom the more solid it is and the lighter it is the more gaseous it becomes. To our prospective everything must have mass which defines the matter as solid liquid or gas due to its density.

Since the atom is in a constant state of vibration that means the realm of the physical is always moving and changing; to understand this concept a little better we see everything according to the vibration of the atoms within the object; furthermore for matter to exist it need to shake really fast for it to give attention for the occupying space where it resides.

This just raise more questions than it answers any, but what we know is that when vibration is slow, things take longer time to develop and when things are sped up they excite and produce a form of energy (heat, light, etc...).

The Laws of Existence

Every state of existence has its own unique "something" that will come to provide and gear up the big machine which is the universe. Existence of animals, plants, rocks, water, earth, ants, iron, gold, air, etc... all need each other and they all work together to exist and maintain the purposeful work piece of the universe.

The presence of all things is the preservation of all; on that notion every state of existence is covered by many laws.

1. Mind over matter: The law of existence of anything must need some kind of information to root the map what the subject will be on the physical plain; this information is the DNA. The connection of the DNA with the waves around us is so important and essentially driven by the need of a higher existence that connects the physical with the spiritual world. The affects that we are talking about here is the law of attraction in the mind of the subject; you are only limited by your imagination and your will to execute the impossible.

2. Universal laws: this category is big but it's all about the physics, chemistry and astrology. Like gravity, kinetic energy, the behavior of the molecules with each other, etc...

3. Divine laws: here all the laws can be broken and be replaced by divine intervention; what we call "miracle" is governed by the most high "GOD" and this has its own laws by itself which GOD only watches over and rule; interventions could be carried by agents of GOD which we call angels and

the cosmic mind has a hand in all the works of the realms.

To be the man of wisdom, you must understand the need for such laws; the prospective limitation of all this physical matter is for a good reason where the guidance of the cosmic mind that is set by GOD must be for all that exists. Chaos only exists when one of these laws is disturbed or disoriented; only divine law is outside the disruptions of chaos.

The Degrees of Life

To understand such a complicated topic we must divide the degrees of life into three different categories; if you understand these degrees you will be able to scale all that is on the degrees of which it is appropriate to its evolvement and involvement in this master piece we call existence.

After much extensive research on this subject, I have found that there are a lot of people discussing these degrees in a different manor with different ideas. The whole purpose of this book is to put forth a solid foundation that makes sense to the reader no hoops and no wiggle information covered with layers of mud; when a purposeful thought comes forth nothing can stop it, and the thought of existence is the purpose in all the degrees.

The degrees of life consist of three main plains:

1) **Physical plain:** on the physical plain we have seven main divisions and each division has also seven sub divisions, this plain deals with all the natural physics and energies.

1. The substances that physics and chemistry of which we know now a days. The manifestation of liquid, solid and gas states of matter. These are the manifestations of matter that is needed for life to flourish.

2. The physical substances with radiation emissions at its natural state. Like uranium, radium etc... this type of matter is always in constant state of radiation without a source or manipulation to their structure. This type of matter is hard to turn off or deal with because it changes the molecular structure of any life form.

3. The physical substances of subatomic particles (not tachyons but other subatomic particles) which the science today just getting acquainted with. For the longest time physics has dealt with matter as particles, but now we are thinking outside the box and treating it as a wave as well as a particle. Here the science of the future will thrive to discover new theories about physics and the exploration of bigger things from one of the smallest things in existence on the matter level. Observation of matter on this level will set the stage for a new era that will bring about the understanding of the physical universe with all its mysteries.

4. Ethereal substances which in definition is light which is the medium of the transference of energy such as light or heat...

5. The energy we know in our physical plain that has much more effect than any other substance; such energies are magnetism, electricity, cohesion, chemical affinity etc... this is the energy that occur naturally, and it is the subtle action of substance and other substances to each other.

6. Forces that exist outside our reach at this moment which the science today call antimatter. We know very little about this element, but it occupies most of our known universe; until we can handle such material it will stay a mystery to us.

7. The highest form of organized energy which is life energy. It has been explained in chapter 6 all about this subject. I will only add that this energy is not recognized by man on the ordinary plain, but it is only available to the spiritual, and mental plains this "chi" is incomprehensible by the ordinary man. Chi energy is only understood by the man of wisdom...

2) **Mental plain:** this plain is all of the mind and the heart. It is the subsequent application of the conscious on all that is. It consists also of seven divisions and each of those consists of seven sub divisions as well.

1. The plain of the mineral mind: it is the lowest realm of the mental mind; everything is alive no matter how slow it evolves. Crystals for example are used in focusing energy because their synergy with our mental mind can help focus the healing of a subject or other influential properties depending on the crystal. The push of this plain makes all the basic structure in the mental stability of things; it's like the anchor in which we ground our self to; and for us to reach the beyond we have to be able to have a grounding point. This is the reason why we use crystals as grounding agents in our meditations; keep in mind that we have to understand how to use them.

2. The plain of the elemental mind #1: there are entities that exist out of the boundaries of the physical that our eye can't see. To put this into prospective that will bring it closer to mind, the elementals we talk about here are of earth, water, air and fire and they exist around the bodies that they are natural to.

3. Plain of the plant mind: this is comprised of all that is to do with the plant world. There have been some scientific discoveries that discuss and recognize that plants have feelings and they response to your input to them. The man of wisdom would recognize that all living things have feelings and a mental mind for it to interact with that of the physical exposure.

4. Plain of the elemental mind #2: This comprises of higher form of elementals which they play their role in the universe between the plain of the plant mind and the animal mind.

5. Plain of the animal mind: This consists in all its parts of the animal kingdom with a degree to each animal species. All animals from the single sense organism at the lowest level (like the snail) to the most complicated and the highest simple minded animals (like dolphins and apes) are bound to the animal mind plain.

6. The plain of elementals mind #3: This is the highest plain of the elemental minds, all its subdivisions partake the forms from the animal mind and that some of the lowest of the human mind.

7. The plain of the human mind: This is where our minds reside it's very important to see where we are on the spiritual scale; when we see the big picture the whole master piece becomes clearer to us and we become elaborate with our work to establish our level on this plain. All humans are covered under these degrees with seven divisions; these divisions consist of the mind degrees of all humans on earth and elsewhere; the average man of today occupy the 4th division of the human mind degree. Although there are some people that are very aware and have passed higher than the given number here, i still think that the average man is on the 4th. I came to this conclusion which is still a

speculation nevertheless; it does make sense where we are now in this age and how advanced we got now let's hope we don't destroy our selves and pass to the 5th without a restart and I bet it will be faster to elevate our selves together which is more productive in becoming what we need to become.

It is important to understand that we always should move forward even if in baby steps as long you move forward you never waist your mind. The mind that thrives forward is the mind of a man who is disciplined, strong willed, knowledgeable of the spirituals, and wise in all his actions.

3) Spiritual plain: it exists beyond the physical and beyond the mental, but it guides them both. Everything happens here first before manifesting on the physical, and the mental is the conduit in which it uses to work the physical. The mental is affected by the spiritual and at the same time the mental can affect the spiritual while the physical can influence the mental, but not affect any spiritual without the mental.

The spiritual plain is the most complicated and the hardest to explain in words we can understand; however I attempt to simplify I will fall short in doing so, now I represent the following understatement of the spiritual:

There are seven divisions and every division has seven sub division as we stated at the start and this follows every plain. We are limited in so many ways to understand this realm because we are not free. There are beings that are very high mentally and in harmony with themselves and the creation. We cannot explain light to a blind man as it is hard to explain the spiritual plain to the ones that hasn't seen it or been there. Here is the rub we all been there between lives but we cannot remember. All angels, guides and light beings exist here in a state of harmony; these beings surpass us in every way even some say they are bathed with light, and since they are super conscious they can come and go to our realm as they please. Every wise man thrives to achieve even the smallest state in this realm so let's try and become the man of wisdom.

Note: *the soul is beyond the spiritual plain; even though it thrives in it like water filling the whole cup everything needs a soul...*

Before we jump into conclusion, we have to mention that each mind has two purposes one is good and one is evil not all can be good and not all can be bad. We on the other hand we have to chose which purpose we should fulfill, keeping in mind that karma plays on all plains with the very intent of thought to re-balance all that is on every plain because they will all be balanced.

Conclusion

There is harmony on all these plains and they work together to serve the whole. It is our purpose to understand the whole while knowing our degree. We can harmonize ourselves with the rest of creation and balance our karma with all that exists. Understanding these plains will bring another big piece of the pyramid into the whole structure of understanding and block by block we will build our own pyramid.

Some stuff might not be so clear at this time to some readers; the most important thing is that now you are aware of how the realms of existence are derived and worked in the most minimal of information to not over whelm anyone. Now we know our place in this world and what our role here is and what degree we are at as humans. Now you have a clear rough map of the whole and you can see yourself taking the first step in becoming the man of wisdom.

Auras & Chakras

Introduction

I did mention in chapter six very briefly about auras and chakras; and that their roles in the human body as the connectors of the spiritual with the physical. Since the application of such knowledge is very important in any spiritual undertaking we have to define the aura and the chakra individually and as a whole. The application of such things in us and around us will guide us to the healing of the body, elevation of the mind and the liberation of the spirit.

Many attempts have been made to explain this subject, but unfortunately a lot have fallen short or incomplete; I am trying in this chapter to put together my prospective on this subject that I have been studying most of my life, and attempt to illustrate to the best of my knowledge" the world of chakra and aura".

The Connection of Bodies

An aura is the unseen non substance body that exists in the spiritual plain around an intelligent body; it occupies the functions and interactions of the physical with the spiritual through guided specific bodies of spiritual substance. These bodies differ from each other in the degrees of effectiveness on the spiritual plain. It is necessary to have these bodies in place around the physical body that they occupy and there are bounded to its spirit. The aura goes with the spirit to another body as it passes from life to life as the spirit separates itself from the soul while departing from the physical body. (Sometimes disease do go on to the next life if the subject still under taking part of the same lesson of the previous life).

Around our physical body there is a series of higher dimensional bodies called aura this aura is made of the following: 1. Etheric
2. Astral
3. Mental
4. Emotional
5. Other dimensional bodies

In our physical body there are wheels of energy that connect the physical body to the aura. These energy centers sprung their name from the eastern traditions and they were called chakras. Each chakra is connected to a vital organ that is necessary to the subject to survive on the physical. The existence of such energy wheels wields the power to be in contact with the spiritual realm at all times. Between the physical and the spiritual there must be a barrier which the chakras play towards the physical side and the aura play towards the spiritual side. This barrier is important so the physical don't get mixed up with the spiritual; the physical has a positive number but the spiritual is a negative number per say. To be clearer, imagine that one to infinity is the physical where anything that has dimensions resides; while minus one to minus infinity will be the spiritual plain, and the zero plus is the chakras and the zero minus is the aura while the actual zero is the barrier.

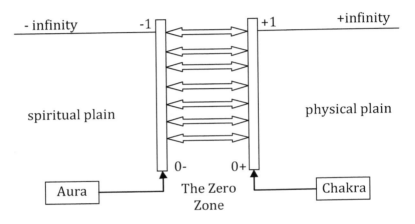

I have explained in chapter 7 that the physical body's essence always must exist on the spiritual realm before it can exist on the physical, and this is a detailed figure of a human essence connected to the aura of the spirit (the self) and then to the wheels of energy (chakras) which in their part drive all the important organs that get the body going on the physical plain.

These energy centers (chakras) are like the UI (user interface) for the aura. This aura has these bodies that are controlled with mental, emotional, astral, etheric and other subtle bodies of the spiritual substance. The aura shapes and connects the chakras to the spiritual realm, and the spiritual realm brings the information or the essence of things from the spiritual and moves it to the aura, where the aura spins these wheels of energy which in their state are naturally controlling the physical body's well being.

With these connections we would have discovered that we are plugged into the big map of the spiritual realm, where everything resides as a mirror to the physical.

The Chakras

Every chakra works at a specific frequency, and attached to a specific gland. In order to have control of the chakras you must have full emotional control and absolute mind discipline. The tachyons that we spoke of in chapter 6 are here in the chakra system these tachyons are exact in the acupressure points that tend to move a specific chakra faster or slower. The eastern medicine use acupuncture treatment contracting on these acupressure points to bring the chakra in question onto balance, and the physical body in its turn becomes balanced as well.

To achieve such a state with the use of mind and emotions, is to bring our self into a trance where you become your true essence and you will be able to access the most inner you.

Through series of breathing exercises you can bring about the balance that we are looking for into every wheel of energy we have the access to.

Mantras and words of power or prayer also can bring the chakras into the right balances of their original state.

Illness and disease are great examples of unbalanced chakras; in an ill body the amount of energy entering and leaving the body is defiantly not correct so it shows on the physical plain. There is no disease in a well maintained yoga body with healthy emotions and a powerful mind. When the chakras spin too fast (over active); an illness would occur from the over active organ when it exhausts itself; the unspent energy have to go somewhere and that's why the chakra becomes over active; when a chakra is under active a disease will replace the healthy tissue to replace the needed energy that is required for that specific organ to operate correctly; this under activeness will make the organ lack in operation that is needed to fulfill the body's need for that organ, and that under activeness will make the body work incorrectly and disease enters the body.

For example when a person's thymus gland becomes over active, the immune system of the body automatically thinks it is under attack and starts to attack the host's own body; the imaginary attack against the body is called an auto immune disease which can attack not just the bones but anything in the body; this extra energy coming from the chakra in question (heart chakra in this case) brings about an auto immune disease called rheumatoid arthritis. An under active thymus or heart chakra will bring about the lessen production of white blood cells, and in this case the host will be very easy to get sick and infections become very common and often. The lack of enough energy going to the thymus gland makes the body fill the gap of emptiness with unhealthy shadowy side, because there is no emptiness only full in existence. So you see that the very act of bringing the chakras into balance makes the gland related to that chakra or affected by it to become normal and just right. This is the art of healing on the very most basic level of understanding.

Theoretically; when you bring these chakras into balance through meditation and other means; the disease gradually should disappear. As you work your meditation on that specific chakra every day, your chakra starts to bring itself back into balance from these exercises as if you are training it to become at that normal energy intake and flow. This has to keep on going until the chakra becomes balanced without the use of the exercises; at that moment the chakra goes back to its "harmony" balanced state as it once was.

chakra	purpose	color	Gland	location	function
Crown	-Spirituality -Relationship to GOD -Universal source	violet	pineal	Above the head	-Circadian rhythms
Third eye	-Intuition -Wisdom -Creative -Intelligence	indigo	-Pineal -Pituitary	C1,C2	-Bodily function Hormones -Physiological regulation
Throat	-Communicate	blue	Thyroid	C3,C7	-metabolism -growth hormones
Heart	-Giving -Receiving	green	Thymus	T1,T5	-Electro magnetic field generator -Blood pressure -Immune system
Solar plexus	-Personal power -Self will	yellow	Pancreas	T5,T9	-Digestion -Assimilation muscles
Sacral	-Survival	orange	Adrenal	T9,L4	-Elimination -Fight or flight response -Water regulation
Base	-Emotional balance -Sexuality -Procreation	Red	ovaries/ testicles	L5,S5	-Reproduction -Growth and Development

Note: Circadian rhythms is the hours of operation in which your daily rhythm of the melatonin production and release in the body. Other words internal clock!

Each disease that enters the body has its root in one of the glands that is associated with that specific chakra. We just mentioned the seven main chakras, but there is a lot more chakras than we know and each governs lesser means of the body. We will only talk about the main chakras and their roles which are very obvious in any human; after we master these chakras and rule over them then we can move on to more complex things for now let us stick to the basics because all derive from there.

The Aura Bodies

Now we have an idea of what the chakras relate to our body, and how an accomplished man of wisdom understand, weave and act on what is needed to make the chakras harmonious with the body. We are prepared to connect the chakras to the aura, and to accomplish that we must define the aura bodies and what they actually represent and how they function.

The aura has specific higher bodies that communicate with a specific chakra which is the door way for the spiritual life force to flow through to that specific chakra. The aura body is the conduit between the chakras and the spiritual plain this depiction is represented in every aura body with chakra entanglement of its representation. To proceed in this direction correctly we will tackle every aura body on its own, and try to understand its place in the big map of the spiritual connections.

The aura bodies:

1. The etheric body: this is the 1st layer of the aura field body. It is directly connected to the lower sustainability of survival and the basic elements of creation; which will bring it to be related with the 1st three chakras :

118

i. The base / root.
ii. The sacral.
iii. The solar plexus.

When a body is about to be conceived this is the 1st body that comes to the imperious. Its information has the basic male/female, structure and the DNA map for that specific person, and also governing planets in the constellation of that person's birth with the destiny intact. At this time the etheric cord is established, and it is a different cord than the mother's etheric cord; we have explained the etheric cord in chapter one I will only add that the etheric cord is the first cord that connects the mind of a person to the cosmic mind, but the mind comes later when the person is about to be born; that cord is the manner of which the spirit will travel to that person (established cord does not mean that the soul is in that imperious, it is later when the soul attaches itself to the spirit and they both will be breathed in when born).

Since we are talking about conceiving; I have to add this note here to help the struggling masses in clarifying the big misunderstood point about sex.

Having more than one sexual partner is not a good thing, because every sexual connection there is a one similar to it in the spirit world; the desire of having sex without falling in love or being in love brings about the entirety of your spiritual degree down. You sink to the lower state of the animal desire within yourself; which makes you more of that state of development rather than being in an elevated state part of your development. It's like if you roam more with thieves you will become eventually a thief and if you roam more with the scientist you are more than likely to learn something. The longer you are in the state of sexual desires the more you feed your animalistic nature, and stay at that state of non love meaningless vibration. It will become harder and harder to get out of that low vibration state, because the more you feed your animal desire the more it wants, and the more it gets too soon it becomes that state. You must become strong, and have enduring patience to train your mind to accept the animal self as an aspect of you that needs to be disciplined, kept in check and follow you authority rather than biting you till you give it what it wants. Taking more than one partner will change your chakras, auras and karma.

It has to mean something for you to give the most sacred to the other person. You must learn them and they must learn you. You both have to be in love for the love to work, because at the end of the road yourself and your partner's self will know each other, and fall in love in such high beautiful cascading outward light of love that you both will feed off until and beyond the grave, and that is true love to the core.

Everything on the physical plain is also affected by the spiritual plain and that whole existence is built on balance between the two. The balance of the spiritual and the physical is the true achievement of the perfect health through respect and discipline of the body. The reason they call the body "the temple of light" is because using this body properly is what makes it possible for this whole system to work in the process of ascending to enlightenment.

2. Astral body: on the 2nd layer of the aura lies the astral body. Before we can learn about the astral body, we must talk about what lays after death.

    In order to understand this subject matter we have to indulge on certain information that is unclear or covered by a lot of fog. To experience death you must die and obviously I am writing this book from this side, so I can only theorize this information to the best of my ability from the sense of logic and information that I have gathered over the years and finally from observations of the spiritual through some meditation sessions. We will tackle this subject from the side of logical disarray. When we talk about death a lot of people run away from the subject, either because they fear death or their fear of the unknown. It doesn't matter how or when you die because that is not in your control, but what really matters is the journey and what you have accomplished.

    The more we dive into this subject the more we have unanswered questions.

    a. Where does our conscious go when we die?

b. Why we can't remember anything from our past life?
c. What does the astral body have to do with death?
d. Is there heaven and hell?
e. Why do we live if we are going to die?
f. What is the state of death?

Everyone is destined to die no matter who they are or what they've done; if you are a priest, an engineer, mother Teresa, Gandhi, the president, a doctor etc... you still have to face the inevitable but what you do, sets you for your next life.

Reincarnation always happens and your guides will find you the right life so you can continue your lessons; if you are in grade 10 they will not put you in grade 8 again; either you move up or repeat your grade.

Some people think that death is an external thing, and when you die that's it that is the end..... But death really is the main axel of the wheel of life; each life is unique each existence is perfection on its own; life and death are the means in which life will produce the infinite number of possibilities where the person is in as many number of play grounds and lessons as possible till that person have achieved ascension.

Without death there is no life and without life there is no death this is the circle of existence....

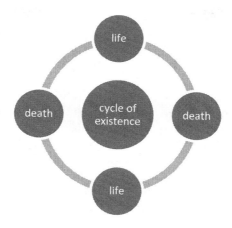

Time operates differently in the spirit world it's like the dream realm; 10 seconds in a dream could be a life time on earth. This is only for the mind not for the body.

People don't reincarnate right away there is a waiting period to say good bye to our loved ones and finishing any business needed to be dealt with (purely non physical business think of it like scrooge Mcduck Christmas revelation understanding the why). Then the deceased will enter the ether realm and meet their guides to see what they still need to work on before they get their next experience.

Some spirits find it hard to move on and they get stuck here. Like they have unfinished business and cannot accept the fact that death has claimed them. We would call this category ghosts.

The spirits also move in clusters or groups and they often help each other through all the lessons to achieve higher states of consciousness and become guides themselves. This is all explained in Michael Newton beautiful informative book "journey of souls: case studies of life between lives" this book illustrates an incredible insight into what happens to us when we pass.

All your life with all your actions, intents, thoughts, deeds and misdeeds, pleasures, cries, and loves that you have had in your lifetime will become energy patterns and build up on your karma. These energy patterns could range from very bad, bad, good, better, and different; these energy patterns will sum up one's life time into one state of patterning and it will be on the scale of feeling. At the moment of death, the final energy patterning state you hold will settle into the astral body and stays there. Here it becomes a little complicated you will leave your physical body, but you are still holding on to the etheric body for the moment being you are still conscious about this life and who you hold dear and who you love and what you love; you get to see them one last time as a mercy thing; here people will OBE to rush and see all that they hold dear to. Some could come back to life if they are saved in the hospital or CPR or other means of a miracle. When dying you will see yourself moving upwards through all matter as if it is water which is an OBE at death and we call it NDE (near death experience).

Note: there is always a prayer that must be said to the deceased in order to help them move on; the deceased will stick around till his funeral is done, and the prayer will help him/her to move on. When you go a funeral you don't say good bye to the physical dead body, but to his etheric presence in the room.

The next thing to happen is the pull; the pull is like a magnet the sucks you toward the white light. The white light is the astral body that pulls you toward your next body this pull is about to take you to meet with your guides before your next incarnation. In Michael Newton's book in the journey of souls he explains of the afterlife from his hypnotized subjects it's a must read to understand this subject more. Furthermore, what will happen to us after that moment it is important to grasp the state that you are in at this stage of life transference. In the astral body the following will happen:

A. If you were a happy person, mostly positive and you died with that good energy pattern this feeling of goodness will be multiplied by 1000 folds and that is called heaven.

B. If you were a greedy unhappy person mostly self pity and you died with that middle ranked energy pattern you are just feeling bad but you are not bad you will just fall back to the same cycle with similar conditions.

C. If you were a bad, evil, harmful person toward yourself and others and mostly negative when you die with that maleficent energy pattern this feeling of hurtful ego will be multiplied by 1000 folds and that is called hell.

Note: heaven and hell are specific state of feeling in the astral body and since the astral body is not physical the feeling is multiplied by 1000.

Each life lived is a focus or a quest for you to better yourself in every way possible. It is very important to consider the condition in which the cosmic mind will rule over any destiny of any person. Where the creator sees all and knows what is best for you in any given situation.

Every moment in your life is preparing you for death from your child hood all that you do in this life time is added to your life pattern of your life force and accumulate all that is "you" in one essence.

If you were a materialistic person you will chase all that you love of the materials and what will you claim but the heart ache of always wanting, and no matter what you get you will always want more. That is a selfish life that no one will benefit from, not even you.

If you love people and give (not necessarily money it could be anything) from your heart you will live a loving life with heart of gold even if you don't own the gold, but you become that love which will feel that you already owned the world and all the gold in it. Spread the love and the world will be a better place for all of us and our children and their children.

If you devoted your life towards the knowledge and wisdom of the ages you won't only liberate your mind and elevate your spirit, but you will influence the people around you to live better in their body, mind and spirit. You become righteous, free, and elevated in heart, mind and spirit into the higher echelon of spiritual degrees. Spread the knowledge and the darkness of ignorance will dissipate and sprout out the flower of wisdom.

There is a lot of "ifs "in each of our lives, but the bottom line is what you do in your life is what truly matters. Circumstances might appear at any moment in your life; to change it, but your acting upon it is what matters your decisions, your opinion, your thinking, your intent and your choice is what will react to your life pattern.

My question is what is heaven and hell? The answer to that question I answered it to myself longtime ago; heaven and hell are states in which your life patterns intertwine with the cosmic law of creation. The state of heaven and hell are very real and they are the law of inter dimension that exist in the spiritual realm, which is related to the karmic law; the cosmic law is on the spiritual while the karmic law is on the physical. All must obey these laws; you can never escape them, or hide from them. As we explained earlier; if you are good your life pattern will be on the happy heaven side, and if you were bad you will be on the hell scale of things and bound to repeat more life time experiences till you learn to have more wisdom.

As we continue in the process of after death here we reach the astral body which is responsible for your threshold of your between lives. The astral world is the land of the dead and the realm of dreams and astral connections. The astral body is connected to your:

      i.   Heart chakra.
     ii.   Crown chakra.

The astral body is very unique and holds the life pattern of you, and it is important to understand the workings that are happening around you for you to achieve the wisdom state in which you will become the man of wisdom.

3. Mental body: it is the mind, that was explained in chapter 1; I will only add that the chakras connected to the mind are:

i.   Throat.

ii. Third eye.

iii. Crown.

The mental body works with the physical body and enhances its experience through the understanding of everything that is in and out of the body physically and spiritually. The mind is the only means that can connect us to the cosmic mind, our self (spirit) and our consciousness all at the same time. These connections will bring about one full mental body that will bring you up in the degrees of spirituality, and furthermore this mental body is the one that will push the self into liberation in the end. To elevate the self into knowing all that is around you and beyond you is the stride of the real man of wisdom; while still in this fragile body you can achieve all the means of the mind.

4. Emotional body: it is where your emotions reside and work. This body links to the following chakras:

i.   Base.

ii. Sacral.

iii. Solar plexus.

iv. Heart.

This body is connected to the astral body, but separate from it; this body is delicate easy to manipulate and stimulate. Emotions should give you the necessary motivation, but never rule over you. Emotions are explained in chapter 2 and all that you need to know at this time is in that particular chapter. You are the master of your emotions at least you should be; your mind should rule them to serve you, and that is the way you make them work towards your advancement. The man of wisdom is the man who rules over his emotions through the mastery of his will.

To gain enlightenment is to make your way of life towards that goal; in everything that you do if it is work, home, socializing etc... you have to live it on every level, and every encounter should be towards that enlightenment. You cannot say today it is ok to hurt people and tomorrow I will go back to my goal; it is a working progress towards becoming the man of wisdom. When you seek to become wise and be it in every action you take and every choice you make with every word that you speak and every thought that you bring forth, you truly would have accomplished the true wisdom; your feelings will come up, and you "the man of wisdom" must be the master in the essence of becoming the man of wisdom.

Mastering your emotions is not an easy task, but to achieve this state of emotional equilibrium, you must accumulate the following virtues of an adept:

a) Your behavior must be exemplary humble and truthful. When your behavior is up to the standard humbleness of a monk; you care not to the materials of the world, but only to the advancement of you and the ones around through truth and peace; your ego have no place to ruin what you have in your heart. The ego is the self destruct magnesium that is in each and every one of us that destroys wisdom with its relentless selfish driven thoughts. This ego runs from pure ignorance and selfish acts, and the lack of wisdom produce egoistic thoughts that will blind the most knowledgeable of people.

b) Your actions must coincide with harmony and respect to self, nature and others. Every action has an opposite equal reaction; from here you should suffice that whatever you put forth you will get back. If you give love you will receive love; if you spread hatred you will only be hated; if you spread the wisdom you will be met with a better world all around you with an initial awareness, and more adequate thinking environment. When your karma is on the right balance of everything you would have completed a very big chunk of your errands and the cosmic mind will help you achieve these goals of yours. All feelings must come from a pure sense of love and devotion, and not because you have to do such acts, but because you want to. Be as it may you are a part of the big picture, and we all are a part of this thing called life thriving to understand all that is with our mind and feel all the experiences with our hearts. Let us make our actions count and have the universe take care of everything else.

c) Your mind and heart must be in sync with each other. All that is in your brain and heart must have a good synchronous connection where they all answer to your mind, but motivated by emotions. It is easy to be blinded by emotions; when you love someone so much it is easy not to use logic no matter what wrong did they do; you just turn a blind eye; here in this fickle of emotion you are guided by feelings and not being wise. Same with anger and other feelings it is easy to lose your grip on your thoughts when emotions run hot. The disciplinary acts of mastering the mind with all its aspects will attain you the mastery over your emotions and your mind will rule them. Your emotions become your weapon and not your act, and your act becomes from thought and you become the man of wisdom.

5. Other dimensional bodies: I will only mention that those bodies exist, and they are part of the soul and other spiritual bodies that we do not know much about. We will conclude that these bodies are in deep esoteric knowledge that we are not ready for yet.

Conclusion

In conclusion I will demonstrate the adept paths towards the actions they chose. In an effort to put forth an adequate understanding what is on the horizon; the new era has begun and the best is yet to come. The best we can do is to get ourselves ready and good things will happen. Auras and chakras are the beginning of a new age of understanding that its roots were in the old age, but for some reason of our ignorance we lost it yet to be introduced again. The best thing to do is to drive our self out of the darkness and not fall in that love and that we all are part of the whole thriving the degree of becoming the man of wisdom.

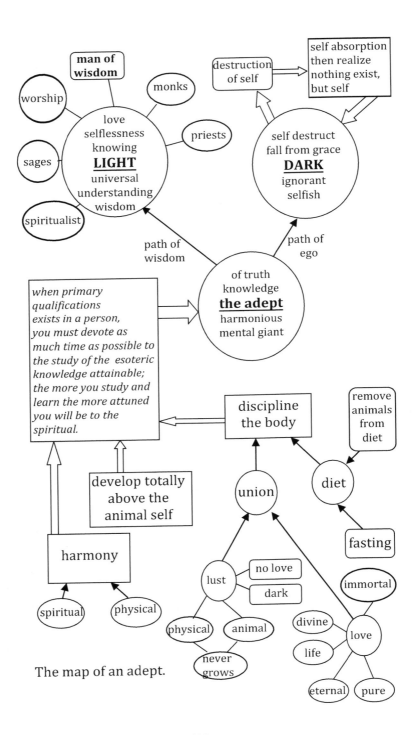

The map of an adept.

Meditation

Introduction:

A lot of people tend to use substances like weed, Ayahuasca, DMT substances or drugs in order to achieve some kind of a bliss. Amongst other experiences, bliss (being high) is one of the experiences of spiritually that is directly connected to the physical senses. Why would use hallucinogens when you can train your mind and discipline yourself to achieve higher spiritual results controlled by you. You become the master of your mind not being mastered by some drug or artificial substance which is only made to stimulate the condition of spirituality not living it (being high is a fake spiritual experience that doesn't help you in any way). What if you can achieve the bliss without the use of drugs? To be in a state of bliss without the use of an agent like drugs you have truly achieved nirvana in all its aspects. The use of a mind altering substance would give the bliss for a period of time, on the long run it does more harm than good and soon you will be dependent on it; then you will reach a point that you cannot achieve anything with the drug.

Alcohol is a different kind of mind alteration; when people drink their third eye starts producing melatonin this will lead the mind or consciousness to be absent and that will lead to other things or entities taking possession of you and your body that's why people wake up places they don't know with people they just met. Were these your actions? Or something has possessed your fragile mind at the time of the drinking?

Meditation is the processes in which you bend you mind to come into a trance where the body follows. Meditation can be achieved through the stimulation of breath while focusing your mind on the object or subject that is of interest. There are many forms of meditations and each person is receptive to different kinds; where every affinity has its housing and every person have many affinities.

About meditation:

Purification is essential to all aspects of spirituality and the purification of the heart, mind and body can attain the healthy manipulation of the spiritual purity of any subject. Meditation is a way to accommodate all these paths of purification on the way to enlightenment.

- Purification of the heart is untangling the hatred in a way to accept all that is just the way it is.
- Purification of the mind is to master your thoughts on a level of connection to the highest state of intellectual wisdom.
- Purification of the body is through fasting and the achievement of good healthy life changing habits (not diets).

Meditation can help you achieve all the above purification goals; with a bit of work, study, execution of principles and regular meditations you will achieve these goals.

The heart is pure when it is full of love and absolutely no hatred. Devotion is one of the ways towards enlightenment; to love completely and unconditionally with no hesitation or doubt is the absolute truth about love. Meditation is one of the ways in which you can see the truth and achieve inner peace; with inner peace you would have uncovered the most important piece of love.

The mind is hard to control, and controlling it is like trying to direct a hurricane to go in certain direction; if you calm your mind it becomes as gentle as a leaf. And to calm the mind is to down size the chatter through the means of meditations, mantras and prayers. Purifying the mind is hard work, and will take time; but you have to start somewhere, and the first step is always the hardest. Purification of the mind through the act of meditation and willing the self not to be selfish, cruel or just plain evil; through meditation you don't only calm your mind you also expand it; you will find new senses which are not of this world. You start to know the essence of things; you will begin to feel the world as it really is and not the illusion that masks it. You will see the whole creation more organized, and everything exist with a purpose and the man of wisdom would know the purpose of things. Everything seems to be in the big wheel intertwining with each other in complex combinations that all start to make sense, and become clearer with every meditation you do. To attain such a stage you cannot chain the mind, but through training and acts of disciplines which will strengthen your will.

Purifying the body through disciplines:

A. Fasting and cleansing on a regular bases to clear all the toxins or garbage we put in our body.
B. Committing to a Vegetable diet is a must to become more pure; no animal products must be used to Norrish the body.
C. Meditation is to balance the chakras in order the body's physicality be balanced as well.

How do you expect to have a chance at evolving into higher spiritual life form if you cannot take care of this body? If you can carry 2 pounds then you shouldn't be carrying 4 pounds for an example; same with your body until you take care of the physical body fully you cannot handle the higher spiritual bodies.

For starters meditation is to leave all senses behind and become senseless; after mastering your mind you don't become senseless instead your senses physical and spiritual become super senses.

When meditation is mastered the self will be revealed.

Use your will to restrain your senses do not chain them, but train them; this will take time but the master of his senses is the master of his mind and the master of his mind is enlightened, and through the enlightened mind cometh the man of wisdom.

Stages of Meditation

Meditation is one of the easiest forms of energy manifestation; the meditation mastery can be achieved through the following stages:

1) Knowledge:

a. What is meditation: meditation is the ability to train your breath to work for you. With every breath you take you stimulate life; when inhaling you intake air and the life force, and exhaling you get rid of the burnt oxygen and release the life force. When shallow breaths are taken not enough oxygen is consumed and the cells will not operate correctly; the question is how many full breaths do you take per day? When you meditate every day even for 20 minutes only you will improve your body health drastically, and that is scientifically proven.

b. How to meditate: the most simplistic way to meditate is to sit in a most comfortable position, and your spine must be straight or aligned and then take your breath slowly in through your nose (not mouth very important) till you fill your lungs completely; then hold your breath for 2 or 3 seconds; then exhale slowly out through your nose or mouth it is really up to you; then hold your breath on an empty lungs for 2 to 3 seconds. Repeat process until you have gotten the rhythm; now focus on a wave that is moving from the bottom of your feet up wards toward your head and every muscle it passes through that muscle becomes relaxed. Every breath you take, a part of your muscles gets relaxed and move up and over all your body till your body becomes relaxed; this is the basic steps of meditation where every meditation out there uses these specific steps that will lead you to further development of your technique in meditation.

c. What to expect: in the light of this new age almost everyone knows what mediation is or what it means in the general sense; the beautiful thing about meditation is that we all do some type of meditation. Every time you exhale deep and inhale you would have done one type of meditation; when you are angry there is something you do to calm yourself when you inhale deeply and exhale after that you lessen your anger drastically that is one type of meditation. The calmest state you will ever be in other than sleep is when you are in deep trance of meditation; when you meditate, your body feels lighter and stress free and all your muscles become so relaxed and your cells become saturated with oxygen. Depending on the meditation you are applying, you will see different results and that will be discussed later in this chapter. After meditation, your mind become surprisingly peaceful or in a state of bliss; the most amazing thing that I notice all the time is when I meditate my energy level increase and each time I did meditation that level of energy increases in occupancy (I can hold more energy) till it becomes as if I am flying. Meditation can help with pain, but the concentration is hard to come by when your mind is distracted by that pain; if you can keep your mind focused on the meditation your pain can be lessened or even disappear in some cases. If there is a problem you couldn't solve whatever it may be, but if you meditate on that problem you will think clearer and your options will be weighed in front of you.

2) Discipline:
a. Kinds of disciplines: there are many kinds of disciplines that any person can learn. Most people tend to go to modern trend for the execution of meditation; such meditations are with yoga which will help you understand your body through series of exercises and technical moves that are meant to give you the means of learning your body, and connecting

it with your mind; these types of postures make up the body to become stronger while under the influence of the mind.

Yoga:

The whole entirety of meditation according to the yoga practitioners is to make the self become the witness not a participant. And I agree it's like when you are doing OBE "out of body experience" you watch your body consciously while you are around it or above it hovering with your mind.

In the Vedas they add "yoga's ultimate purpose is to reshape our self to become more pure and clearer to our selves through our will" and this adds to the importance of meditation and practicing it till mastering the body through the mind.

Yoga literary means union; to define the different paths of yoga is necessary to understand one of the most renowned practiced disciplines in the world today. The yoga is of four different paths and they are as follows:

A. Karma yoga: the yoga of action.
B. Raja yoga: meditation, discipline.
C. Yana yoga: the yoga of wisdom and knowledge.
D. Bhakti yoga: devotion.

Other disciplines like kung fu, tai chi (personal favorite) and many more were made to discipline the mind and make the body bend to its will. The body becomes stronger and thought processing becomes faster with these disciplines at the same time the body become more fluent and the movements become like a beautiful dance that is just right.

Although all these schools of discipline have different but great things to offer in the terms of mind and body communications; you don't need to participate in these schools to meditate, but you have to discipline yourself to meditate regularly to increase your potential. The art of meditation is to go into that inner peace as fast as you can (not forcing it; it has to be natural); which is where you find your wisdom.

b. Fasting and cleansing of the body: to put forth all the possibilities that you can achieve; the tools that you need to use must always be healthy, strong, reliable and sharp. To achieve such a state; fasting and cleansing must be taken as a life style choice, and to improve in every stage of life as necessity demands. Fasting and cleansing will bring about the new you at every corner shining to improve on every stage, and that is the power of health and health is the highest level of wealth.

c. A must for meditation: there are certain things that must be taken into consideration before meditation, during and after. They are as follows:

    A. No food for two hours before meditation.

    B. No alcohol, drugs, or any mind altering substances.

    C. A place that is quiet no back ground noise.

    D. Sit or lay any way you like however you are comfortable as long as the spleen or back is straight.

E. Cleansing the place of meditation is a must (use incense or sage or sweet grass even just a candle would suffice)
F. No interruptions.

3) meditating:
a. Pick a clean place, and quiet with no interruption as mentioned previously; you can use incense or sage for cleansing; meditation in nature is ideal. The first step in meditation is grounding yourself and this is done in many ways; the most important thing is to remember that grounding is a term used to holster your mind to an objective ideal state that will act as an anchor in order to stabilize your ground here on the physical. There are many ways to ground:

    I. Using crystals is a beautiful way to ground yourself; usually people use base chakra related crystals, but you can use clear crystal quartz which is ideal for cleansing.

    II. The use of a pre meditation that is grounding in its own nature before the actual meditation; all you have to do is 10 minutes of basic meditation technique while visualizing your base or feet as a tree that its roots goes down deep into the earth.

    III. Grounding through another person; while in group meditation the group members keep each other grounded.

    IV. The use of an object with special relation to the subject; the object can be anything from a totem to a piece of wood or rock or even a ring. The object can even be an artifact or religious book that the relation with that person is strong as steel.

    V.   A special place that has close relation to the person; this special place can be a spiritual or religious retreat or special religious place like a church or a mosque or even a prophet's visitor centre ... etc

b. Types: there are many kinds of meditation and all depend on the purpose of the meditation. There are meditations for cleansing energies, protection, focusing, clarifying a subject matter, clearing head, calming mind (very important), balancing chakras, healing, medium ship, energizing, remote viewing, unlocking potentials, accessing the mental and emotional bodies, mind exploration, dream meaning, etc... I don't think there is a limit of how much you can do with meditation. Meditation can also be generalized just for relaxation and that is ideal for starters.

General meditation is so powerful that if done correctly and constantly you can accomplish:

    A. Physical changes to the neurons in the brain.
    B. Elevate your vibration.
    C. Mastering all the senses.
    D. Realizing life's purpose.
    E. Lucid dreaming.
    F. Knowing past lives.

G. Mind over matter realization.
H. Cleanse the self.
I. Knowing thy self.
J. Exploring and analyzing personal dream.
K. Prayer or mantra with meditation is 10 folds more powerful.
L. Unlocking the potentials of your mind.
M. Organizing the mind.

Astral projection is one of the most beautiful mediations that would:

A. Travel beyond physical limitations with your mind "remote viewing".
B. Increased psychic abilities.
C. Witnessing other realities.
D. Exploring other realms.
E. Understanding the point of view of death and beyond.
F. Contact of the higher self.

c. Guided meditation: for starters it is good to do guided meditation either with a group or just through a teacher or a guru or even just an experienced meditater. The experience from these encounters will help you build your confidence in doing it yourself; the group meditation will raise the vibration of the space around the people involved very high where all will feed of off. The guided meditation will use a right method that is proven to work, but later you will make your own technique which will suit you.

d. Your own: there is no one way of doing meditation, but there is a principle of meditation that all expand from. After a while from experiencing others technique of meditating; you will certainly must develop your own; for every prospect of thought there is a kind of meditation you can do. The potentials of meditations grow exponentially as you grow spiritually and your limit is what you want to be. The only limit you have is what you set yourself to; expand and grow and your understanding of the universe grows with it.

When you master your breath you will rule your body.

Self check

You and your guides are the only ones who know what aspect of progress you can do for your spiritual advancement.

You have a choice between right and wrong, and choosing the right path even if the right path was easy you are going to advance spiritually to a higher level of thinking. What you face in your life only makes you stronger or weaker and all depends on your success or fail; the only thing that matters from all your fails is to learn how to do things differently and learn from them; you will thrive in becoming a higher advanced spiritual being when you broaden your thinking.

"I have not failed. I've just found 10,000 ways that won't work." Thomas A. Edison

What we are talking about here is that the harder the challenge the bigger is the trophy. The easier the challenge the smaller the trophy becomes. Whatever you chose will affect you in the long run; if you pick the hard road it is more rewarding but it will be rough. You should challenge yourself on every corner as much as you can that is how you advance faster.

Hard challenge:

- ❖ If you succeed your advance rate is➔ 10/10.
- ❖ If you fail but trying hard your advance rate is ➔ 4/10.

Easy challenge:

- ❖ If you succeed your advance rate is➔ 5/10.
- ❖ If you fail but trying hard your advance rate is ➔ 1/10.

You will always get something for trying.

There is a reason and purpose for everything you do at the now of every thought in any place; realizing that truth makes you the observer of your purpose; at that moment and in that thought you become the man wisdom. The moment you realize your purpose in every situation you become wisdom itself and you will ascend only higher in the spiritual evolution.

As explained in detail in chapter 8, chakra is a Sanskrit word which means wheels of energy; our body holds 7 main chakras that govern the spiritual energy flow in and out of the body. It is the wheel of the spiritual attraction or the pin point of the crossing between the physical and the spiritual. Each of these chakras is a key to the spiritual connections through our aura, and each chakra plays a major role in the meditation disciplines. For every chakra there is a purpose and the control of these chakras can come through meditation; which is why every spiritualist has a unique signature meditation that is private to their own development.

In the long effort to become the man of wisdom you have to find your own signature that is private to you; I will give some examples of my own experience with meditations in the purpose to illustrate a further view into the world of meditation.

My Meditation Examples

You are responsible to do your work, and in this chapter it is very important for you to build your own spiritual attitude. Meditation will set the degree of your inheritance of energies that is going through your chakras, and that will set your aura in the right patterns for spiritual evolution. The evolution is the elevation of your spirit or the self into the echelon of the spiritual realm. The higher you get the higher your wisdom will become.

1. Cone meditation:

   Fill the body with light and healing energy. This meditation is the best before sleep energizes you for the next day and will get you in a deep trance of calmness.

   *conditioning:

   1. Lie down on your back.
   2. Start breathing meditation {inhale: 4 sec hold: 2sec, exhale: 4sec hold: 4sec}.
   3. Repeat till almost in trance.
   4. Thinking of calming your brain and lessen the thought process as much as you can.
   5. Numbness and floating feeling takes over your body completely.
   6. Draw a circle in your mind around your body.

7. Like a cone where the base is beneath you and the pinpoint is perpendicular to your body directly above you.

8. Every inhale a shower of light comes in from that pinpoint straight through; it starts moving spirally clock wise till it envelopes all around you descending to the base and fills the cone completely with light swirling round and round.

9. Every inhale you take; the body grasps on to the light and where the oxygen you are inhaling fills every limp in your body so will the light.

10. Now visualize the light entering your nostrils with every inhale and filling more and more energy into you.

11. When you exhale the body will let go of the excess energy back into the cone.

12. Do as many as you like of inhales and exhales until your body is full of light.

13. Left and right hand are at 90 degrees with your body open palm and feel the energy that's flowing through your body.

14. Do as many as you think you need and when exiting this state counter clock wise the light back through the cone where it came from.

2. Balancing chakras as a whole:

Balance all the chakra by using shocking breath from abdomen, this meditation is perfect for untwining knots in the chakras and trying to balance its spin. This meditation is for minor disruptions in the chakra system and won't work on big twines. But a good day to day healthy meditation chakra balance; this meditation is for the wonderful natural flow of energy onto the physical body.

*conditioning:

1. Lie down on your back or sit in a comfortable position.
2. Start breathing meditation {inhale: 4 sec, hold: 2sec, exhale: 4sec hold: 4sec}.
3. Repeat till almost in trance.
4. Thinking of calming your brain less thoughts.
5. Numbness and floating feeling take over the body as it gets enveloped in the trance.
6. Now take a 1 deep breath {inhale: 6sec hold: 2sec}.
7. Exhale in short breath from the bottom of your stomach while moving your stomach short exhale for each inhale about 10 exhales. "Note: this might not be easy but practice until you get it right."
8. Every breath of those deep ones look at one chakra in your body and watch it untwines.
9. Repeat as much as needed till you feel the balance.

3. Quick rejuvenation:
This meditation is the perfect meditation for uplifting of energy level or refills your power levels; while giving you clarity for a short period of time. It is perfect for use at work or any place that you cannot hinder your attention for more than 1 or 2 minutes.

*conditioning:

1. Standing up right hands straight down.
2. Start breathing meditation {inhale: 6 sec, hold: 2sec, exhale: 5sec, hold: 2sec}.

3. With every inhale lift your arms in a circle up till they are up right pointing to the ceiling.
4. With every exhale put down your arms in a circle downright till they are pointing to the floor.
5. At the top of the inhale blank out all thoughts of work or personal feelings of whatever you are performing.
6. At the bottom of the exhale think of your muscles being relaxed to the state of numb almost or completely relaxed for that 2 brief seconds.
7. Your whole body should tinkle with sensation to all the limps.
8. The top part of the brain should feel like a rising sensation going from the tip of the ear to the top of the head and then a little pressure builds up going in a circle moving inward toward the centre of the head.
9. When that happens, repeat the process for about a minute and exhale finally exiting the meditation.
10. You will be fully heightened in the senses and the mind is clear and sharp; and the whole process should take a few minutes maximum depending how fast you can achieve the trance.

These two meditations amongst other meditations have been developed by me to suit or establish a certain function for my purpose. Every once and a while I have to create a new meditation out of necessity in order to solve a problem or to execute a spiritual experiment.

Conclusion

The struggle of human beings with their restrains of the physical world, and the ties that hold humans out of freedom is the cast of their mindlessness towards things with no purpose. For the man to rise spiritually he has to break all these restrains and make his mind and spirit free.

The whole universe is working according to a rhythm and a very precise calculated order; why you want to be out of this order. You have to realize that what you are doing, and ask your self is this order or chaos. When you see the world as a big whole giant puzzle and you are just a small piece of this puzzle and you are a part of the solution you become harmonious with nature and the universe; that will put you on top of the spiritual game which is essential if you want to become the man of wisdom.

A meaningful life is to live your life in understanding reality in its diversity and complexity.

The Theory

The Break Down

At an atomic level, the laws of physics and the structural behavior of the atom have been set and then left to interact with one another; where this randomness doesn't work on the molecular level as it does on the atomic level for this stage of creation the cosmic mind comes into play to set the elements through the molecules activity and behavior. On the grand scale of things the physical manifestation of solids are the clusters of molecules that make up matter and all its differentials; where every element is defined and given characteristics for it to be unique. In the alchemical traditions, each element is said to be ruled by a planet of its nature; like mars for example, rules the element iron and the sun rules the element gold and so on and so forth. To understand this subject more clearly we have to understand that there is nothing left for chance but the atoms themselves in their behavior to one another, but in a cluster of molecules the atoms act as one as if they are one entity belonging to the element they are in.

Albert Einstein said "GOD doesn't play with dice", when the big bang occurred and the universe was created the clusters of galaxies scattered all across the universe; in the midst of all that chaos and the pulling of the elements, earth came to be in our milky way galaxy in a perfect position from our sun where it is not too hot to fry us or too far for us to be frozen, and out of nowhere it accumulated an atmospheric shield that will protect any life form that might happen and make it plausible to thrive. Does this sound like random?

The rocks falling from space does not seem to be random anymore; they have been on a course through space for millions of years and earth stumbles on their path through sheer course interception and definitely not chance. The universe might have started with a big bang, but the perfect evolution of the galaxies through the universe carrying these planets in a perfect harmony with each other where all exist together just doesn't seem to be random.

Now here is a good question.

Why can't we say that evolution did happen, but with guidance and control from a higher power (GOD)?

Evolution is the form of advancing forward towards better state of living while survival of the all is through the change that must happen or it will perish. In Darwin's theory of evolution there are too many farfetched ideas and it stays as a theory just like the theory I am representing here. In my opinion, if Darwin's theory was right then we simply cannot see monkeys today because we would have been all of them. Monkeys have developed their own evolution and they became the monkeys we see today, and we have come from something else all together; we might have looked like hairy humans, but we were humans from the start.

Darwin's evolution theory is not a proven fact that there was any change of kinds; this is a quote from the Darwin theory of evolution's web site where they state "That is, complex creatures evolve from more simplistic ancestors naturally over time. In a nutshell, as random genetic mutations occur within an organism's genetic code, the beneficial mutations are preserved because they aid survival -- a process known as "natural selection." These beneficial mutations are passed on to the next generation. Over time, beneficial mutations accumulate and the result is an entirely different organism (not just a variation of the original, but an entirely different creature)"

http://www.darwins-theory-of-evolution.com/

Here is that word again "random", when we talk of a random genetic mutation a cat cannot transform into a dog or a snake into lion or a fish into a bee or a bird into a rat. So how we first came from a fish I can never say, but for me it DOESN'T AND WILL NOT MAKE SENSE. Darwin's theory is broken and there is no scientific evidence that nature works that way. Nature works in a progressive elevation of all that is in it to suit the grand cosmic mind's vision of the whole; when GOD gave the cosmic mind the plans for evolution to take place it was not up to chance that life found root on this planet we call earth; it is the conditions that the cosmic mind set for this planet. It is safe to say that evolution happened with "the kind" through the advancement of all species each kind on its own.

The thing about random mutation they cannot occur without an input from an external source that gave it that push to evolve. The responsibility of the cosmic mind is to make sure that all that is needed for the spiritual and physical advancement is to be provided and cared for, and that can occur when the cosmic mind make the changes by influencing the physical through the means of the manipulation of the atoms within the cell of the organism; as if the cosmic mind gave a push for evolving and then watch the outcome as it unfolds.

To see the whole picture more clearly, I have put the theory into prospective and will try to explain my idea as much as possible by dividing the creation into categories and explaining each as an entity by itself and where we stand in all this.

My Theory:

Guided evolution has occurred.

Evolution happened with the mind and spirit; in the previous chapters of this book I clearly explained how all the physical is a mirror of the spiritual and all have to occur on the spiritual realm before entering the realm of the physical. The spiritual evolution happened to all within the confinement of the mind.

The Way of Evolution:

1. The minerals:

The minerals are the rocks and all that is still to the most basic form of chemistry in nature. Some might say that rocks or a diamond or any kind of mineral doesn't have any spiritual connection. Well think about this way every rock or amber or any kind of quartz has a direct connection to the spiritual world, because it can resonate with a specific frequency that can be used to access a specific chakra or alter the mind's state of focus.

The chemistry and the physical structure of these rocks will remain the same until they are changed to something else; the change of the element can come from the influence of something physical upon it, or the change in the structure of its magnetism due to an unseen force. In the esoteric teachings of alchemy where the change of the base metal to become gold is exactly the ladder of spiritual evolution that I have been trying to point out; where the base metal is you in the most simplistic state of mind then your efforts will transform you to be golden like the highest rank of the mineral or shall I say enlightened?

A cluster of carbon atoms under super pressure will become a diamond; imagine the changes that are happening all around us that we know so little about.

Is it safe to say that the world of the spiritual enlightenment has started since the first atom took its shape?
Would you agree that for an evolution to occur there has to be enough reason for it to happen or even to exist?

Well I will tell you that at one point in time we had the simplest of minds just like a mineral is; when we are ready, all we have to do is just move on from the stillness toward the start of the spiritual evolution that will only advance us on the ladder of creation.
At this level of consciousness you will recognize matter and what it is at its true form, a still born entity.

2. The plant:

Plants are the first form of an emotion string towards nature and its evolution. Plants are the clusters of life force ready to commit expansion almost mindlessly. The plants are faster than rocks to evolve spiritually; this will make the food on the physical plain for everything to follow animal and human.

The consumption of food will give us energy to sustain our existence. When you use animals flesh as a food source you will take in chi energy from an animal which in extension committing used chi energy to move into you, but when you consume the plant as a source of food your chi will be getting pure chi and not mudded through the flesh of another.

At this level of consciousness the plants are the first step towards "the moving life" and this beautiful evolution is one big step from stillness to basic stirring. This basic life form will set the stage where all can exist in the simplest form possible.

The plant kingdom is the first act of giving on the spiritual level. Without the plant kingdom none can survive let alone to advance anywhere; the very act of giving gives this world a new perception of the positive proposition for the sake of nature's expansion.

Nature is built in code; this code has been set as the structure of the nature's law where GOD puts it in order to build this world; there must be a formula where all can follow for the structure not to fall apart. This law or code is embedded in every living thing no matter what, where or who they are; if you want to exist on the physical world you must follow this code. This code is the golden number of nature which is called "the spiral" also referred to as "Fibonacci sequence". This golden ratio can base all nature's forms which require not a straight line or a dot, but something a little more complex like the spiral.

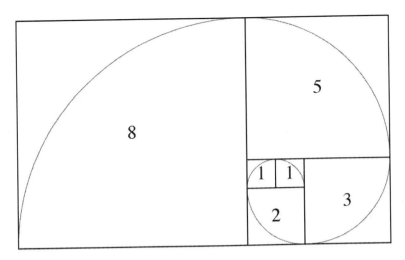

This golden ratio is all over basic life in nature you can say that this ratio is the global number that nature uses to execute life in building things.

Golden ratio = Phi = 1.618

The golden number is between 1 and 2 or 1.618 as it gets more refined as the creation gets more complex, because it will need that level of detail. For example a leaf is less complex than that of a kidney in the structure of its creation.

Although the plant kingdom might be simplistic to the rest of creation, but without the giving of the plants we can never thrive; the plant kingdom is the base that hold this structure we call life together.

3. Animal:

Here comes the first form of the physical brain in its lowest form in nature; from the snail at the lowest to the dolphin and monkey at it's highest. Animals are born with the brain that already is knowledgeable of survival built in to it.

For example let's say a baby goat was just born and you try to push it off a rock it will resist and try to hold on, because the survival brain is built in and no need to gain the knowledge of survival or to understand danger; while with a human baby the limit to potential knowledge is limitless, but it needs to be gained, because to fill the human brain you need to learn; when a baby human is born it knows nothing of this world and the information of danger has yet to be gained because it is not built in. That is why humans have never been monkeys; sure that monkeys or dogs or cats can learn tricks, but they still have the animalistic given brain nothing new can be acquired or invented with these brains they are committing for treats.

Monkeys are the highest form of the ANIMAL spiritual evolution that's why THEY LOOK LIKE US, and NOT THE OTHER WAY AROUND.

The animal kingdom is the first plain where nothing is given to you, but you have to take it by force and survival of the fittest is the game; where all prey on each other to survive.

The animal in the spiritual world is needed to reproduce by the interaction between the male and female of the given species; to understand the animals a little more we have to view this logically. As we know, animals have only a specific time in the year to reproduce and it's a time preset that is built for them and impeded into their brain; where humans follow no such internal presets for the sexual orientation. That just proves that animals are given a brain not to think, but purely submissive to direction not intellectual.

The animal kingdom is always in survival mode while spiritual growth is dependent on the inner piece to surpass the internal struggle between animalistic nature and pure intellect, we find ourselves in the need to surpass these animalistic behaviors and seek the self's ascendancy above the animal self.

4. Humans:

We are the top of the spiritual chain as far as we know. We are defined by the mind that holds all of our intelligence and knowledge. This knowledge we are not born with but accumulated through trials and learning experiences which is all explained in chapter one of this book; I will only add that we are absorbers of knowledge and creators of theories and the inventors of our age. Animals don't have cities and schools and hospitals; our advancement in all the fields of intellect puts us on the top of the food chain; not because we are stronger, but because we have a mind that is able to advance and expand. The thing about spiritual evolution is that it is still happening now and will continue to happen till the end of time; if it doesn't progress it will die and if that happen there is no purpose to life.

Evolution happened but it happened through mind & spiritual advancement from a monkey kind of MIND to a human kind of MIND. The man of wisdom is the man who went through all these steps of evolution and elevated himself to become an adept of spiritual being, and beyond.

Conclusion

A theory stays a theory, but the spiritual evolution is what matters to us and our advancement becomes wisdom itself.
The dominos effect is the well established system of reaction to a purpose, where the ripple of dominance of the entire creation will be affected in the spiritual sense; the behavior of the creation to that chain reaction is always in constant

motion to accommodate the cosmic mind's inner structure; where the effect of one thing will lead the events of new things, and so on so forth. The behavior of all that is, is the outcome of the cosmic mind's influence on that which is physical.

The purpose of evolution is to move forward in all the aspects of its entirety and make sure the upcoming of it is nothing less from the original either same or better.

The Drop of Wisdom

The Bhagavad Gita clearly explains that wisdom is the highest way to GOD, and devotion is the shortest way; to put this in prospective; devotion is the shortest and hardest way to GOD because it is the utter unconditional love and complete devotion unhindered where there is no doubt to the absolute certitude of love to GOD and his creation, where the most highest grace is achieved; if you can achieve that state of devotion that will be the shortest way. In the process of accumulating wisdom though, you would have imparked on a quest to understand devotion as well as attaining wisdom; that is why wisdom is not just feeling but feeling and thinking; the man of wisdom is the man that tries to understand GOD and his creation; he understands how to love GOD and all that is with a purpose; he admires the way that the universe is constructed and how it works while seeing a purpose to everything there is to be.

The way of wisdom is the way of understanding the beyond; see all that is, be all that there is to be. Become the knowledge you learn and execute its virtues in every corner of your existence that is the man of wisdom. Expanding your mind to swallow the whole with understanding; see the prospect of things from many sides and forge opinions based on experience and knowingness.

Wisdom is accumulated like knowledge, but the difference is that wisdom is the essence of knowledge and all the feelings that comes with it; the true knowledge is the knowledge where it aligns with the heart and mind. Do not fret if you haven't acquired wisdom yet, wisdom will find you with time and your spiritual worth will set it to you.

Philosophy and wisdom are close to each other in so many ways; Philosophy is the study of a subject in which all sides of the argument can be right, while wisdom is the right way of understanding things; wisdom is the elevation of any subject above philosophy to its spiritual essence, or you can say that philosophy is the base of wisdom. The attainability of wisdom is impeded into our core; just like gold ingots, it will not shine its true nature until it is purified with fire over and over to become pure, and the fire is the trails that we endure to become our true wisdom self.

Some might say that this world is a world of materialism, deception, hatred and misunderstanding; a trap where people get ensnared with all the physical materials that drives the wanting to more wanting no matter how much they have, where jealousy kills friendships and lies become the truth just because it is convenient. The real world is nothing of the sort; only for those that are weak, ignorant, close minded and evil see the world in this image; their mind is not seeing the beauty that is in all creation; they have created the prison which they can never leave, but it is of their own making. If this world was really a trickster, then man at the start of time would have been happy; until one time when something goes wrong and he gets hurt then the pain comes out and bring along the misery where happiness fades away to never return. Our conception of emotions and our entanglement with them will set our state affairs of the type that we ought to be, and we bring the happiness that we seek or the misery of which we fall upon. The truth about this world is that when we are born here each of us will face different conditions that will either gives us strength if we are strong willed or fall into despair if we are weak. This world is not evil nor good it is the outcome of how we perceive it, where a person would see a jungle full of danger and death, and others would see it as a diversity of beautiful creations that is full of life; if a person always think of this world as possession then this world in his conception will be an opportunity where everything becomes a commodity. The man of wisdom will seek virtue in everything he does; he is the definition of an elevated spiritual philosopher that seeks the betterment of himself through the elevation of his mind.

The big question here is how can we elevate our mind?

The first step toward our betterment is to be in control of our mind; we have to guide the ship of our understanding to the calm shores of action. Everything that must be executed in action must be crystal clear to us before imparking on any task. Angered people lose their grip on their actions and they fail to use their mind and fall from grace through the actions of outburst and rage.

What is anger and where does it come from?

Anger is nothing but the invasion of one's personality; when a person is in a deep state of meditation he is alone with no inputs from this world or anyone that is in it; that's why when in trance you feel complete tranquility and freedom and the complete opposite of being mad.

When do we get angry?

To anger someone is by jeopardizing their privacy:

1. Privacy of mind: the invasion of an opinion and the control of one's thinking and the private state of mind and manifestation. The total over whelm of one's decision and clouding it in doubt and frustration.
2. Privacy of space: the invasion of one's home, car, country and anything that he cares for on a materialistic level.
3. Privacy of action: invasion of one's freedom through restricting the freedom of action.

When dealing with a situation that someone has wronged you; you have to take a deep breath and think calculated actions and punish in a calm ethical way by making them understand how they wronged you in an effort to explain the actions that they took did harm to you. This way you will gain their respect and their apology (This doesn't work with ignorant egoistic people and the best thing to do is not to associate yourself with these kind of people).

Understanding people gives you the key to unlock the understanding of peace; you don't have to understand them completely but understanding their simple top part of their mind. The top layer of the mind is enough for you to deal with them in most good sense of way. Understanding how to read people will get you the best outcome of any relationship; in doing so you will always be in the light where you shine on people with love, because you understand them and know them in some aspect.

How not to hurt others?

Imagine yourself in their situation unless you visualize their situation you can't understand what they are going through; never ever judge people and their way of thinking, they have their path and you have yours. Never try to change someone's opinion that's their opinion and not yours; make sure you hear their opinion and respect their decision even if it's not true; maybe your opinion is wrong, and maybe they are not at the level of knowledge that you are at. You have to let them grow on their own till they accept the truth in any form it may come.

Pay attention to your actions and always think; don't let your tongue think for you; think logically check it in your heart and then let you tongue do its job. Understand each situation and deal with it as required with passion and commitment to act from the heart.

Free your spiritual life

To live a life of happiness through the inner peace that nothing should bother you no matter how dramatic and hard life gets. This is a hard discipline to achieve but the acting on our betterment and evolving our self will get us there someday. How to be happy? This is a big question and the way to approach this is by dealing with the source of what makes you sad and miserable "losing things of value, pain and disease, not having what you want etc..." it's not all these things that make you sad or mad it's how you feel about them. The master of his own mind will conquer his feelings not by rejecting them but by disciplining the self in accepting them and learning them. You are the man of wisdom that is in control of his emotions through his disciplined mind.

We must honor the spirits of our ancestors and their way of life; never forgetting that we are evolving to the better but they were the start of this mind evolution.

To live in the freedom of likes and dislikes so you can attain certain calmness that will get you to your betterment. Free yourself from the influence of others, you have your own thoughts and mind; never follow a man always get the knowledge that you need and learn the truth by doing the work yourself; think on your own and become the example for others. Free yourself from the stuff you want make sure it doesn't rule over your life, most of us still stuck at that point in this grand deception of retail; break free and become the independent thinker that can't be tempted by the industry of I want a new phone, I want new car, I want I want ....

Break free from the state of mind delusion and lies. Become the Truth knower not just a seeker and break all ties to the grand deception of politics in everything we do; let us put an end to the influence of war and control. If we are all free from this there will be peace on earth; follow your heart's intuition and your mind's logic don't believe everything they tell you always count on your hearing and seeing in real time. Media deception, government cover-ups and all in between are just stuff made to make you fail your ascension and be stuck here in this illusion. To have an opinion you have to have your thinking free and unhinged and not guided; guided opinions is the opinion of another mind and not your own and this opinion is someone else's idea.

Meditation and prayer are very important and they are the back bone of the ascension we are trying to attain. You must want to meditate not force yourself you will get nowhere in forcing, but you have to allow it to come through to you and let it take you to a world of calmness and peace where you have only one thought; where the flow of energy from the divine showering you and you becoming one with the divine. Intense prayer is as powerful as meditation and it all depends on your intent and the essence of will and love.

Being lazy and ignorant doesn't help us in any way; instead it will slow or even halt our spiritual development, as a matter of fact authority figures take advantage of this to maintain their power and influence over us. All the information is under our fingertips nowadays because of the internet; everything is very convenient, and we don't have to travel thousands of miles to get a spiritual education all we need to do is to stop our laziness and start educating ourselves into the knowledge to become the man of wisdom and help our children in their journey and get them attached to the spiritual expansion of the mind; they are our future and if you get them on a good ideology from the start; they will become leaders one day and do the change that this world desperately needs.

The action life like doing your regular job and all your daily things and how you react and learn from them you will get the right playground to ascend even maybe faster than a monk because you chose the life of action and the monk chose the life of non action your tests can be done sooner. The monk got the time that you don't have so which will you chose. Devotion to your own duties like taking care of your family and doing your work in a good will get you on the right way to your spiritual awakening, but this is incomplete you still have to do your homework to refine your mind... if you are ignorant of the spiritual wisdom you are deemed not to be worthy of the information and the knowledge and it will not be shown to you.

Refusing to do your work that's intended of you or running away from you responsibilities will get you on the lower scale of spiritual ladder and sink more deep in to the material war that's happening to everyone. True intention is giving without expecting anything in return, loving without condition and learning with good intention this is how you free your ego.

Even if you kill someone and your intention is trying to save them, you will be judged for intention and not the result (and that's in the spiritual world). The knowledge when to act and when to watch and do nothing is the essence of the true man of wisdom.

Order and Chaos

Confusion never lead to change, but it will lead to chaos. Knowledge is power, and the right knowledge will bring about the right kind of forward moving of any change. When ignorance is bound to the person; then the change is all in chaos and forced to happen which is negative kind of change, and that might lead to a positive change eventually after a whole shake up of the prime foundations. If change didn't happen after the chaos, the person will sink lower into the hole of materialism and the sickness of ignorance; sinking lower will only produce a downhill spiraling further down into darkness of ignorance uncontrollably, but at the moment that this person realizes the fal and open their mind into the possibility of positive thinking and willing the change of their heart lead by their mind, they will start to climb the ladder of spirituality out of ignorance in rapid pace on to the light. Through knowledge and love a person will bring about the positive healthy thinking that will eventually bring the person onto ascension.

Unlocking your potential of understanding these subjects is a must to become the man of wisdom; the question is how long it will take you to get to that understanding. When this level of knowledge has been unlocked and achieved you will have the potential that your "will" will shift mountains.

Without any delay you must start your work on your betterment today if you didn't already; there is no reason not to have fun and entertain your self, but never let that get in the way of your advancement into something profoundly bigger.

Your foundation is your ability to fit all the understanding that you can accumulate into one big system that is right for you; where your potential is harnessed and well sharpened to become the "you" that want to be the man of wisdom.

On that note I will conclude this book with good hearted well wishing to all in all endeavors, and I hope everyone will reach their dreams and manifest them into their mind and project them onto this world.

BIBLIOGRAPHY

Freke, Timothy and Gandy, Peter. The Hermetica: The Lost Wisdom of the Pharaohs. 2002

Burgoyne, Thomas. The Light of Egypt: the science of the soul and the stars. 1889

Athene's Theory of Everything published on January 2011 on you tube through the channel AtheneWins link: https://www.youtube.com/watch?v=dbh5l0b2-0o

Newton, Michael. Journey of Souls: Case Studies of Life Between Lives. 1994

Made in the USA
San Bernardino, CA
02 December 2017